Sylvia Barbara Soberton

The Forgotten Years of Anne Boleyn:
The Habsburg & Valois Courts

GOLDEN AGE PUBLISHING

Copyright © Sylvia Barbara Soberton 2023

The right of Sylvia Barbara Soberton to be identified as the Author of the Work has been asserted by her in accordance with the Copyright, Designs and Patents Act 1988.

All rights reserved. No part of this publication may be reproduced, stored in a retrieval system, or transmitted, in any form or by any means without the prior written permission of the publisher, nor be otherwise circulated in any form of binding or cover other than in which it is published and without a similar condition being imposed on the subsequent purchaser.

ISBN: 9798862286113

This book is dedicated to my husband, Mitja, and our children, Amanda and Evan.

Contents

Prologue 1

Chapter 1: Childhood at Hever Castle 3

Chapter 2: "La Petite Boulain" 11

Chapter 3: Mademoiselle Boleyn goes to France 28

Chapter 4: Life at the French court 36

Chapter 5: The legend of Briis-sous-Forges 71

Chapter 6: Serving Queen Claude 81

Chapter 7: Anne's last years in France 115

Chapter 8: "More French than a Frenchwoman born" 129

Chapter 9: Back in Calais 153

Chapter 10: "Very expert in French tongue" 165

Chapter 11: "French bringing up and manners" 179

Chapter 12: "Le Royne Anne sans tête" 189

Appendix 1: In which year was Anne Boleyn born? 193

Appendix 2: Was Mary Boleyn Francis I's mistress? 199

Acknowledgments 204

Picture section 205

Selected Bibliography 218

About the Author 227

Prologue

In 1536, shortly after Anne Boleyn's execution, Henry VIII refused a potential French bride and observed that he had had enough of "French bringing up and manners", referring to Anne's Continental education. In her lifetime, Anne was said to have been "more French than Frenchwoman born", and in her death Henry VIII granted her the mercy of being executed by a French executioner instead of an English one, who would butcher her "little neck" to pieces. This executioner from Calais who wielded a two-handed sword was, however, ordered before Anne was put on trial for adultery, incest and treason, making it clear that her death was a foregone conclusion. Anne's rise and fall is a tale of love and loss, religion and spirituality, queenship and power. The final years of her life are well known, but her youth remains an understudied topic.

Anne Boleyn was raised in Belgium and France, spending seven years at the most glittering and progressive courts of Europe. Her mentors were the most brilliant and fascinating women of the sixteenth century. It is from them that Anne received a spiritual and humanistic education and learned how women could wield power and use it for greater good. When she returned to England, Anne was equipped with knowledge and Continental gloss that most of her female contemporaries lacked.

In this book, I will take you on a journey through sixteenth-century Belgium and France, showing you where Anne Boleyn spent her formative years and introducing the royal women she served. What places did she visit? Who were the women who mentored her and impacted her outlook of the world? Whom did she emulate when she became queen in 1533? All of these questions are answered in this book.

Chapter 1:
Childhood at Hever Castle

In 1536, Anne Boleyn's father would reminisce that his wife "brought me every year a child" when his father was alive.[1] William Boleyn, Anne's grandfather, died on 10 October 1505, so this means that some of the Boleyn children were born before that date, most likely in Blickling Hall, the family seat in the county of Norfolk. The exact year of Anne's birth remains unknown, with historians arguing that she was born either c. 1501 or c. 1507. The present author believes this to be an inaccurate and outdated narrative that does not reflect everything that the primary source material tells us about Anne's early years. It is more accurate to state that Anne was born between c. 1501 and c. 1505. Further discussion of why these particular dates are chosen is explained in Appendix 1.

The Boleyns moved to Hever Castle in 1505, so Anne and her siblings grew up in Kent. New research conducted at Hever Castle by historian Simon Thurley shows that the castle was built in 1383 for John de Cobham, not in 1270 for

William de Hever, as was previously thought. Previously it was believed that the Long Gallery was added by Thomas Boleyn and was thus known to the young Anne, but Thurley's research reveals that the Long Gallery was added by Anne of Cleves, Henry VIII's fourth wife, who resided at Hever following the annulment of her marriage to the King in 1540.[2] Thurley's research also highlights how well-preserved the castle is; the gatehouse and battlements are original to the 14th century as well as the unique portcullis mechanism.[3]

Hever Castle served as the Boleyn family seat from 1462, when Anne's great-grandfather Geoffrey Boleyn purchased it from Sir Thomas Cobham, until 1539, when Anne's grandmother Margaret Butler died there in her mid-seventies. In 1903, American investor William Waldorf Astor started transforming Hever Castle into what it looks like today.

The Boleyns traced their origins to Geoffrey Boleyn, who was born in 1405. He started his stunning career as a hatter in the 1420s, later becoming a successful merchant and joining the Mercer's Company in 1436. He became an alderman for the Castle Barnard Ward, and in 1446 he became the Sheriff of London. Geoffrey's career reached its peak in 1457 when he became the Lord Mayor of London.

Geoffrey married twice. His second wife was Anne, the daughter and heiress of Lord Hoo and Hastings. Geoffrey's son William married the daughter of the seventh Earl of Ormond, Lady Margaret Butler. William and Margaret's son Thomas Boleyn was born around 1477. He married Elizabeth, the daughter of Thomas Howard, Earl of Surrey, who became the second Duke of Norfolk in 1514. The dukedom of Norfolk had come into the Howard family in 1483 when John Howard was created the first Duke of Norfolk. John Howard lost his life beside Richard III in the Battle of Bosworth Field in 1485. Although his title should have passed to his son Thomas, the Earl of Surrey, Henry VII, who defeated Richard III at Bosworth Field, stripped him of his lands and sent him to the Tower of London. After three years, the Earl of Surrey was released and pledged his allegiance to Henry VII. He was eventually created the second Duke of Norfolk, and this title passed on to his eldest son, Thomas, the brother of Thomas Boleyn's wife, Elizabeth.

Anne Boleyn shared a nursery with four siblings. She had an elder sister, Mary, and three brothers: George, Thomas and Henry. Only Mary and George lived to adulthood; both Thomas and Henry died young. Their memorial brasses commemorate their deaths and are the only evidence they ever existed. Henry is buried at St Peter's Chapel near Hever Castle while Thomas rests in the Sidney Chapel at Penshurst Place. It's interesting to speculate why Anne Boleyn's forgotten brothers are buried in these chapels. Henry probably died after the family moved to Hever in 1505. He could have been the oldest child born to Thomas and Elizabeth Boleyn since he is named Henry, after the King. Thomas the younger may have died c. 1522 because he lies buried near Penshurst Place. Thomas Boleyn was appointed as keeper of Penshurst Place by Henry VIII following its reversion to the Crown after the execution of the property's previous owner, Edward Stafford, third Duke of Buckingham. Thomas made renovations at Penshurst in 1525 and stayed there in August 1528 when he was recovering from the sweating sickness. In a paper entitled *Penshurst Church: The Hidden History*, J.A. Flower suggested that Thomas Boleyn the younger was born at Penshurst after his father became keeper, so this means he may have been born as late as 1522 or after that date.

Little is known about Anne Boleyn's childhood at Hever or her early relationships with her parents and siblings. There is no trace of Anne's mother in the service of Queen Elizabeth of York, wife of Henry VII and mother of the future Henry VIII, so it is plausible that she devoted her time to childbearing and overseeing her children's education. Tudor mothers were responsible for teaching their daughters a variety of skills and behaviours, such as reading, writing, needlework, keeping household accounts, riding and dancing. The Boleyns were a great family in the making, and they almost certainly employed tutors to teach their children. Thomas Boleyn was a skilled diplomat and an excellent linguist, and his later care of his daughters' learning points to the fact that he had high hopes for Anne and Mary and afforded them the best possible education.

Elizabeth Boleyn's natal family, the Howards, patronised poet John Skelton, and it is possible that Anne Boleyn's mother appreciated poetry and strived to teach her children the same appreciation. Both Anne and her younger brother, George, were known for their love of poetry, with George being noted for his skill in that department, although none of his compositions survived. We may assume that history was among the sciences taught at Hever because Anne's elder sister, Mary, admitted later in her life that she read "old books" recounting tales in which kings and queens pardoned those who had offended them.[4]

In *Memorials of the Howard Family of Corby Castle*, printed in 1834, Henry Howard stated that Anne Boleyn's mother died at Lambeth of puerperal fever on 14 December 1512. Writing later in the nineteenth century, the eminent Victorian historian Agnes Strickland repeated this assertion and added that Anne's father had remarried to "a Norfolk woman of humble origin".[5] Writing in 1880, S. Hubert Burke asserted, with a great deal of confidence, that Anne's stepmother "outlived her husband and stepchildren many years" and lived "in a cottage near London" after Anne's death. He also claimed that Queen Elizabeth "has never visited or enquired after her step-grandmother", although he provides no proof of such allegations.[6] It is interesting to note that none of these authors provided the name of Anne's stepmother. Today we know that Elizabeth Howard Boleyn did not die in 1512. It was her younger sister, Muriel Howard, Lady Knyvett, who died of childbed fever that year. In fact, Elizabeth outlived Anne Boleyn by two years, dying in 1538.

The available evidence suggests that Anne Boleyn was close with her mother because in a letter to her friend she remarked that "next mine own mother I know no woman alive that I love better", hinting at a warm and loving relationship.[7] It is also evident that she took pride in her mother's Howard ancestry. This is clearly visible in George Cavendish's story about Anne's relationship with Henry Percy. Both Cardinal Wolsey and Percy's father believed that Anne, "a simple maid, and having but a knight to her father", was not a fitting match for the Earl of Northumberland's heir. Percy defended Anne's descent, arguing that "by her mother she is nigh of the Norfolk blood".[8] It is highly likely that Anne and Percy had prepared beforehand to defend their relationship and that Anne felt that, although her father was merely a knight at the time, she had a very prominent ancestry through her female relatives.

Anne Boleyn's childhood ended in 1513 when her father secured her a position within the household of Margaret of Austria in the Netherlands. A slender, dark-haired girl left Hever Castle that summer and crossed the Channel for the first time to spend her formative years abroad, far away from family. She would come back home eight years later, but she would never be that same Anne Boleyn who left in 1513.

NOTES

[1] *Letters and Papers, Foreign and Domestic, Henry VIII,* Volume 11, n. 17.
[2] https://www.hevercastle.co.uk/news/hever-castle-rediscovered/
[3] Ibid.

[4] Barbara J. Harris, *English Aristocratic Women*, p. 166.
[5] Agnes Strickland, *Lives of the Queens of England*, p. 198.
[6] S. Hubert Burke, *Historical Portraits of the Tudor Dynasty*, Volume 1, p. 175.
[7] Eric Ives, *The Life and Death of Anne Boleyn*, p. 23.
[8] George Cavendish, *The Life of Cardinal Wolsey*, p. 123.

Chapter 2: "La Petite Boulain"

In June 1513, Anne Boleyn's father returned from a successful embassy to the court of Archduchess Margaret of Austria in the Netherlands.[1] Thomas Boleyn had great news for his daughter Anne: he had succeeded in securing her a post as maid of honour to the archduchess. We do not know Anne's reaction to this news; she may have been sad to leave her family and depart to an unknown land, but, at the same time, she may have been excited to have a rare opportunity for education and social training at the court of one of the most powerful women of the time. We do not know why Thomas Boleyn's choice fell on Anne. Most historians agree that although Anne appears to have been younger than her sister, Mary, she was a fast learner and a promising child.

Margaret of Austria was born on 10 January 1480 in Mechelen to Maximilian I of Austria and Mary of Burgundy, which means that she was about three years younger than Anne's father. She left her family home at the age of three and was brought up at the French court because she was engaged to the French King's son and heir, Dauphin Charles.

The marriage never came to effect, however, and in 1491 Margaret's father demanded the return of his daughter and her dowry. Anne of Beaujeu, who ruled France as regent at the time, refused to release Margaret who stayed in France until 1493.

In 1497, Margaret married John, Prince of Asturias, son of Isabella I of Castile and Ferdinand II of Aragon. She left her homeland for Spain, where she met her sister-in-law Katharine of Aragon, who would become her lifelong friend. The marriage turned out to be a happy union, but John died within six months, and Margaret miscarried their only child soon after. Margaret's miscarriage was a blow to her in-laws, who hoped for John's posthumous heir. Peter Martyr wrote: "Instead of the desired offspring, she has aborted; instead of the longed for heir, we have been given an unformed mass of flesh worthy of pity."[2]

Margaret left Spain in 1499. Two years later she married Philibert Duke of Savoy, whom she had met at the French court several years earlier. The couple was happy together, but Philibert died in 1504 at the age of twenty-four, leaving Margaret a childless widow. In 1507, Margaret became the regent of the Netherlands during the minority of her nephew, the future Holy Roman Emperor Charles V.

The exact date of Anne Boleyn's departure to Margaret of Austria's court is unknown, but we may assume that her father sent her there soon after his return home in the early summer of 1513. In her letter to Thomas Boleyn after Anne's arrival, the archduchess recorded her first impression of her new maid of honour:

"I have received your letter by the Esquire Bouton who has presented your daughter to me, who is very welcome, and I am confident of being able to deal with her in a way which will give you satisfaction, so that on your return the two of us will need no intermediary other than she. I find her so bright and pleasant for her young age that I am more beholden to you for sending her to me than you are to me."[3]

While the archduchess's first impression of Anne is well recorded, we do not know what Anne felt when she set her eyes upon her royal mistress for the first time. The first lesson Anne might have learned upon meeting "Madame Margaret", as the regent was known throughout the courts of Europe, was that external beauty was not all that mattered. Margaret had a protruding jaw, thick lips and large nose. Her most becoming feature was her curly golden hair tinged with red, although she was constrained by etiquette to hide it beneath a headdress. At thirty-three, the archduchess was not a beauty, but she had cultivated a carefully constructed image of a powerful, if humble, woman of positive temperament and considerable intelligence. At first glance, she might have cut a rather sombre figure in her widow's apparel, but this was just a ploy devised to underline her status as an influential woman, *feme sole*, as only widowhood gave women opportunities to operate independently of men.

Closer interaction offered a window into Margaret's cheerful personality. Antonio de Beatis, who visited Margaret's court in 1518, wrote that she was "not ugly at all" and had "a great and truly imperial presence" as well as "a certain most pleasing way of laughing".[4] Margaret certainly had a sense of humour, as attested by several English ambassadors, including Anne Boleyn's father, who shook hands with her on a bet that progress in their negotiations would be achieved within ten days. If she lost, Margaret was to give Thomas Boleyn a fine Spanish courser; if he lost, he was to present the archduchess with a small horse commonly referred to as a "hobby".[5] Margaret often engaged in humorous banter with foreign ambassadors and enjoyed telling "merry tales". Her laugh must have been very pleasant, as one of the English ambassadors recorded that "she laughed heartily, after her accustomed manner" on one occasion.[6]

It is striking that after so many vicissitudes of fortune Margaret maintained a positive disposition. Raised at the French court as a child-bride of Charles VIII, she was jilted after eight years and left France with a feeling of enduring resentment. In 1497, she married the son and heir of Isabella of Castile and Ferdinand of Aragon. John, Prince of Asturias was a frail teenager who died within months after the wedding. Margaret was devastated and miscarried her child a few months later. Her next husband, Philibert, Duke of Savoy, died young, leaving Margaret a widow at twenty-four. She endured these tribulations with remarkable dignity and adopted a surprisingly modern motto: "Fortune, misfortune, strengthens one [Fortune infortune fort une]."[7]

Margaret of Austria held her court at Mechelen in Brabant. The so-called Savoy Palace, named after the domain of Margaret's third husband, was extensively renovated when she moved there in 1507. This first phase of renovation lasted nine years and ended in 1516. The second phase started in 1517 and lasted until Margaret's death in 1530. Antonio de Beatis, who visited Margaret's residence in July 1518, left a detailed description of the town and palace:

"From Louvain we went to lunch at Malines [French name for Mechelen], four leagues away. It is a very large walled town, very strong and fine, with the broadest most beautiful streets we had yet seen, paved with small stones placed upright and sloping towards the sides so that they retain no water or mud. The chief church [St. Rumbold's Cathedral] is very beautiful, with a square in front of it longer and much wider than the Campo dei Fiori in Rome; this too is paved in the same way as the streets. Inside the town there are many canals with tidal waters, for they eventually reach the sea."[8]

The palace itself was "very fine and well-appointed though not particularly imposing".[9] The inventory of 1523-24 made very detailed references to the living quarters of the Archduchess Margaret and allows us to have a glimpse inside her luxurious residence. Thanks to these valuable references, we can also follow in the footsteps of young Anne Boleyn and see what she saw when she first arrived there. Eight rooms can be identified based on the 1523-24 inventory: the chapel, the library, the "premiere chambre" (gallery), the "riche cabinet" (reception room), "the seconde chambre a chemynee" (bedroom), the "petite cabinet" (study), the "cabinet empress la jardin" ("room on the garden") and a special space designated for jewels and plate.[10] Although the terms applied to each room do not always indicate its functions, scholars made an attempt to deduce the purpose of each room based on its contents. The premiere chambre, decorated with hangings of blue and yellow taffeta, housed a large number of portraits and little furniture; it is believed to have been Margaret of Austria's portrait gallery.[11] The thirty portraits displayed there depicted Margaret's family and allies and included portraits of Henry VII and Katherine of Aragon.[12] The reason members of the Tudor dynasty were accorded places in Margaret's gallery is because in the 1510s they were her family's allies.

In 1505, there were plans of marriage between Henry VII and Margaret of Austria, and there was the customary exchange of portraits between the couple. The portrait of Henry VII holding a carnation, a flower associated with marriage, is currently stored in the National Portrait Gallery in London and is believed to have been a portrait from Margaret's vast collection.[13] Although the marriage negotiations came to nothing, Margaret remained on friendly terms with the Tudors, and another marriage treaty was arranged. In December 1507, Henry VII's younger daughter Mary Tudor was married by proxy to Margaret of Austria's nephew and ward, Charles, Prince of Castile. Mary and Charles were then eleven and seven years old respectively, and the decision was made that Mary would be sent to the Netherlands in 1514.[14]

As to the portrait of Katherine of Aragon in Margaret's collection, the two women knew each other well because Margaret was briefly married to Katherine's brother, John, and spent three years in Spain after his death. Margaret taught Katherine the French language, and the girls became close friends.[15]

Apart from portraits, Margaret's gallery housed a number of objects from the New World. An inventory drawn in 1516 listed "two boxes of cloth" and "a pair of ladies' shoes" from "the Indies".[16] Margaret was a keen collector of New World objects, and by the time her second extant inventory was drawn seven years later, her collection was much larger, enriched by the gift of New World artefacts she received from her nephew Charles in 1523.[17]

Another public space was Margaret of Austria's fine library, housing her extensive collection of manuscripts, paintings, sculptures, maps, genealogies and more items from the New World. Margaret was an avid art collector and dabbled in painting herself, and she took a great pleasure in displaying her vast collection to the elite visitors who flocked to her cultured court. Jean Lemaire de Belges in his *Le Premier Epistre de l'Amant Vert*, written in 1505, uses the voice of Margaret's pet parrot, her "green lover", to describe Margaret's multiple talents. "I well like to see you sing and laugh/ Dance, play, both read and write", says the parrot, adding that Margaret also painted portraits and knew how to play and tune the monochord.[18]

She had many court painters, including her favourite, Bernard van Orley, whose portraits were faithful depictions of Margaret. The archduchess avoided unnecessary flattery in her portraits and wanted them to reflect her true appearance. When the great German painter Albrecht Dürer showed Margaret his portrait of her father, the archduchess conceived a strong dislike for the piece since her father looked nothing like himself in it. Dürer later recorded that Margaret "so disliked it that I took it away with me".[19] Estonian painter Michel Sittow was also member of Margaret's household; he found an employment with her following the death of his patron Isabella of Castile in November 1504. Sittow created two works of art for Isabella; *The Assumption* in c. 1500 and *The Ascension*, both painted for Isabella's altarpiece, known as *Retablo de Isabel la Católica*, "the only works that Sittow is known to have painted for the *Retablo*".[20] The magnificent *Retablo* was still unfinished upon Isabella's death in 1504, and its forty-seven panels were dispersed; thirty-two were acquired by Margaret.[21]

The library was the main public area of Margaret's palace, and she took a particular delight in showing it to visiting scholars, artists and other distinguished travellers who came to see her. Antonio de Beatis was clearly impressed with the space and described it as "a rich and highly decorated library for women" with books written in French and "bound in velvet with silver-gilt clasps".[22]

When the inventory of Margaret's goods was drawn in 1523-24, there were 379 manuscripts in the library, including maps and printed books stored on twenty labelled shelves.[23] These inventories give us a glimpse into Margaret of Austria's literary tastes and allow us to imagine what kind of books Anne Boleyn could have come across in the archduchess's library. Besides countless missals, breviaries, lives and legends of the saints, prayer books and other traditional religious texts, Margaret owned other books as well. From the titles in her library, we learn how large and varied her taste in reading was; she was interested in history (Froissart's *Chronicles*, *Chronicles of England*, *Commentaries of Julius Caesar*), geography (she had "two world maps on parchment"), genealogy (*The Genealogy of All the Kings of France*, *The Genealogy from Adam to Jesus Christ*), natural history (*The Nature of Birds*), novels (*Lancelot of the Lake*, *The Round Table*), prophetic works (*The Book of Merlin's Prophecies*) and suchlike.[24] As one of Margaret of Austria's eighteen maids of honour, Anne Boleyn had an unlimited access to the library, where she could read these books, gaze at the magnificent portraits of European royalty and admire the stunningly lifelike busts depicting the young Margaret and her third husband, Philibert. The 1516 inventory shows that the library housed twenty paintings "hanging around the fireplace"; Anne would have recognised the portrait of Henry VIII, the King of her own country, who would become her husband one day.[25]

In order to read the books in the archduchess's collection, the young Anne had to learn French. A single letter from her girlhood survives; it was written to her father from Margaret of Austria's summer retreat at the castle of Tervuren near Brussels. The letter, written in French, reveals the teaching methods employed by Anne's tutor, Semmonet:

"Sir, I entreat you to excuse me if this letter is badly written: I can assure you the spelling proceeds entirely from my own head, while the other letters were the work of my hands alone; and Semmonet tells me he has left the letter to be composed by myself that nobody else may know what I am writing to you."[26]

The Semmonet mentioned in Anne's letter was her French tutor. Writing in the nineteenth century, historian Agnes Strickland mistook the Semonet of Margaret of Austria's court for Simonette, French governess to Thomas Boleyn's children. As a result, many novels depict Simonette teaching Anne French at Hever but this has no basis in fact.[27]

Historians agree that at this stage Anne was "not very far advanced in her course", but the references to her earlier letters in French point out that she was making steady progress.[28] In her letter, she assured her father that she was bent to "continue to speak French well and also spell, especially because you have so recommended me to do, and with my own hand I inform you that I will observe it the best I can".[29] When she was not diligently learning the language, Anne attended the archduchess in her private moments. An inventory reveals that in Margaret's bedchamber there was a four-poster bed with curtains, a private altar, a desk and several cupboards. The adjoining study contained several desks and writing tables, books and writing utensils.

Although she didn't have children of her own, Margaret was a foster mother to her late brother's daughters and son. Philip the Handsome married Katharine of Aragon's elder sister, the mad Queen Juana of Castile. They had six children together before Philip died unexpectedly in 1506, aged only twenty-eight. Ferdinand and Catherine were brought up in Spain, while the other four lived at Margaret's court. They were Eleanor, born in 1498; Charles, born in 1500; Isabella, born in 1501; and Mary, born in 1505. All of them would become important figures on the international political stage.

Anne came into daily contact with these young Habsburg heirs. Charles, Prince of Castile, stood out the most. He had a "long, cadaverous face and a lopsided mouth (which drops open when he is not on his guard) with drooping lower lip". Despite this obvious lack of beauty, he exuded royal dignity; "his aspect nonetheless has decorum, grace and great majesty in it". "As for his physique", observed an eyewitness, "he is tall and splendidly built, with a neat, straight leg, the finest you ever saw in one of his rank, and . . . no mean horseman".[30] Charles's favourite sports were hunting and archery. Later in her life Anne's favourite sport was archery as well, and it's highly likely that she learned it at the court of Margaret of Austria.

On 11 June 1514, Anne witnessed the wedding of Margaret's niece Isabel of Austria and Christian II of Denmark. It was a proxy wedding, meaning that a representative of the King of Denmark stood in for him during the ceremony. Isabel was only thirteen years old, and Margaret was adamant that the girl should stay with her until she would be mature enough to leave for Denmark and embark on the role of a wife. In a letter to Maximilian, Margaret wrote:

"The parties assembled on the said day between ten and eleven o'clock, with as much state and honour on our side as was possible, owing to the short notice, in front of the great hall of this house, where Monsieur de Cambrai gave the promises and performed the espousals by word of mouth, as was right between the King of Denmark . . . and Madame Isabel, my niece, whom it certainly did one good to look at. The said promises given, they went to hear high Mass in this hall; and the ambassadors were seated according to their rank, he of Spain beside Monseigneur, to the great content of all, but those of England were not there because 'on ne les scavoit accorder'. And when evening came, supper was served and every one sat down in order, and after supper there were dances and tourneys until very late, when they retired to put the bride to bed as is the custom amongst great princes. Thus all was very solemnly and duly accomplished, to the great delight of the said ambassadors, who thanked me very much at their departure; as they had fulfilled their mission they were anxious to hasten their return, and I believe they will guard your honour and that of this house as much as possible."[31]

Margaret was very close with Isabel and did not want to part with her. Isabel referred to Margaret as "my dear aunt and mother", hinting at a warm and intimate relationship akin to that between mother and daughter. The regent's other niece, Mary, was not as close to Margaret. In May 1514, Mary left her aunt's court and made a perilous journey towards Hungary, where she would marry the son and heir of Vladislaus II of Bohemia and Hungary. She was only nine years old when she left the safety of Margaret's court and made her journey into the unknown land.

Anne Boleyn would soon leave Margaret of Austria's sophisticated court as well. She apparently made quick progress in French because on 14 August 1514 Thomas

Boleyn wrote to Archduchess Margaret from Greenwich Palace asking her to release his daughter, whom he affectionately called "La Petite Boulain"—"the little Boleyn"—from her service.[32] The reason behind this request was the changing of political winds. Henry VIII had broken the alliance with the Hapsburgs, and instead of marrying his sister, Mary Tudor, to Charles of Castile, as was agreed upon, he decided to marry her to the French King, Louis XII. According to Thomas Boleyn, Mary Tudor had specifically requested to have Anne Boleyn in her entourage, and he admitted that "to this request I could not, nor did I know how to refuse".[33] Anne Boleyn's sojourn at the court of Margaret of Austria thus came to an end after fifteen months, but she would never forget her Habsburg mentor.

NOTES

[1] Margaret had many titles. In her letter to Pope Julius II in 1524, she signed herself as "Archduchess of Austria, Duchess of Burgundy and Countess of the Franche-Comté, Dowager of Savoy", and she retained this signature until the end of her life.
[2] Peggy K. Liss, *Isabel the Queen: Life and Times*, p. 367.
[3] Eric Ives, *The Life and Death of Anne Boleyn*, p. 19.
[4] *The Travel Journal of Antonio de Beatis*, ed. J. R. Hale, p. 86.
[5] *Letters and Papers*, Volume 1, n. 1338.
[6] *Letters and Papers*, Volume 4, n. 1322.
[7] Today we would say: "What doesn't kill you makes you stronger."
[8] *The Travel Journal of Antonio de Beatis*, ed. J. R. Hale, p. 86.
[9] Ibid., p. 92.

[10] Dagmar Eichberger & Lisa Beaven, *Family Members and Political Allies: The Portrait Collection of Margaret of Austria*, p. 229.
[11] Ibid.
[12] Ibid 236
[13] Ibid., p. 237.
[14] There were plans for Mary's stay in Margaret's court in 1509 because this issue was discussed in the correspondence between Margaret of Austria and her father. [*Correspondance de l'empereur Maximilien Ier et de Marguerite d'Autriche*, Volume 1, p. 240]
[15] *Calendar of State Papers, Spain,* Volume 1, n. 203.
[16] Deanna MacDonald, *Collecting a New World: The Ethnographic Collections of Margaret of Austria*, p. 654.
[17] Ibid.
[18] Dagmar Eichberger & Lisa Beaven, *Family Members and Political Allies*, p. 253.
[19] *Literary Remains of Albrecht Durer*, p. 121.
[20] Chio Ishikawa, *The Retablo de Isabel la Católica by Juan de Flandes and Michel Sittow*, p. 67.
[21] Susie Nash, *Northern Renaissance Art*, p. 236.
[22] *The Travel Journal*, p. 93.
[23] Dagmar Eichberger & Lisa Beaven, *Family Members and Political Allies*, p. 239.
[24] *Correspondance de l'Empereur Maximilien I et de Marguerite d'Autriche,* Volume 1, ed. Le Glay, pp. 468-477.
[25] Dagmar Eichberger & Lisa Beaven, *Family Members and Political Allies*, p. 241.
[26] Henry Ellis, *Original Letters*, 2nd series, Volume II, pp. 10-12.
[27] https://anneboleynnovels.wordpress.com/2012/08/01/simonette-the-governess-vain-shadow/
[28] Hugh Paget, *The Youth of Anne Boleyn*, p. 167.
[29] Henry Ellis, *Original Letters*, op. cit.
[30] *The Travel Journal*, pp. 89, 90.
[31] Eleanor E. Tremayne, *The First Governess of the Netherlands, Margaret of Austria*, pp. 130, 131.
[32] *The Manuscripts of J. Eliot Hodgkin*, Fifteenth Report, Appendix, Part II, p. 30.
[33] Ibid.

Chapter 3:
Mademoiselle Boleyn goes to France

Asking Margaret of Austria to release his daughter from her service was not an easy request for Thomas Boleyn to make. He regretfully wrote to Margaret that "to this request I could not, nor did I know how to refuse". Thomas knew Margaret would be offended by Henry VIII's betrayal of their alliance. Mary Tudor had been betrothed to Margaret's nephew, Charles of Castile, since 1508, and was referred to at the English court as "Lady Mary, the Princess of Castile".[1] Margaret firmly believed that Mary would soon become a member of her family, and they had started corresponding. One of Mary's letters to Margaret is still extant. She addressed her as "my good aunt" and requested Margaret send over some patterns for new clothes in the Habsburg style. Mary wrote:

"And I have received the pattern of the clothes that the ladies are wearing near you that you have sent to me for which I thank you greatly. Because for a long time I have had the desire to know how the ornaments and clothing that are used over there will fit me and now that I have tried them I am greatly contented with them. Hoping that it will be an easy enough thing for me to leave my accustomed way of dressing when I will find myself with you. Requiring you, my good aunt, that it will please you to make my humble recommendations from me to my very dear and well-loved lord my lord the prince, to whom, and to you, my good aunt, God give good life and long and happy prosperity in all your affairs."[2]

It was a common practice for highborn women to adopt the clothing styles of their husbands' dominions, and Mary's request seemed to confirm that she too believed her match to Charles was inevitable. Margaret was disappointed to see the alliance with England broken, especially because she nurtured a dislike towards the French for discarding her as the bride of Charles VIII when she was a child. The speed with which Henry VIII discarded the Anglo-Imperial alliance stunned Margaret to the point that she refused to believe that Mary Tudor was to become Queen of France and said it must be only a rumour.

In early 1514, soon after Anne of Brittany's death, Margaret herself was offered as a bride for Louis XII, but she refused to remarry. Her niece Eleanor was also a potential candidate, but Margaret refused to marry Eleanor to Louis, arguing that, at sixteen, Eleanor was too young to marry and have children. Henry VIII had no such qualms and decided to sacrifice his eighteen-year-old sister's happiness for the sake of the Anglo-French alliance.

Thomas Boleyn was embarrassed to ask Margaret to release Anne from her service. In his letter, he addressed Margaret as his "very dear and most redoubted lady" and thanked her for the honour of allowing Anne to reside at her court, recommending his further services as Margaret's humble servant.[3] Why Mary Tudor specifically requested Anne Boleyn to join her entourage remains unclear. It has been suggested by several historians that it was Anne's command of the French language that earned her place among Mary Tudor's maids of honour. This is certainly likely since, although Mary was born a princess and had access to the highest levels of education, her command of the French language was poor. It was later recorded by Cardinal Wolsey that Mary wasn't fluent in French and had to rely on her English ladies-in-waiting and translators, who had better language skills.[4]

Another factor in choosing Anne was that a host of her relatives was designated to accompany Mary to France. Almost forty noblemen and women were chosen to go with

Mary to witness her marriage to Louis XII, including Anne Boleyn's paternal grandfather, Thomas Howard, the second Duke of Norfolk, and his second wife, Agnes.[5] The duke's children—Thomas, Earl of Surrey, and Anne, Countess of Oxford—also went to France. It is plausible that Anne owed her employment in Mary Tudor's French household to her Howard relatives. Mary Tudor's entourage set forth from London towards Dover on 19 September 1514. "There is no talk of war here, everyone for two months past being occupied with entertainments and jousting in honour of the departure of the Queen", wrote Lorenzo Pasqualigo on 23 September 1514, describing Mary's appearance and entourage in great detail.[6] The new Queen of France was "accompanied by four of the chief lords of England, namely the Treasurer, the Lord Chamberlain, the Chancellor, and Lord Stanley, besides 400 knights and barons, and 200 gentlemen and other squires, with their horses". Women were on display according to Pasqualigo: "the lords, knights and barons were all accompanied by their wives, attended by their damsels." Pasqualigo, clearly impressed by the spectacle, enthused:

"There would be about 1,000 palfreys, and 100 women's carriages. There are so many gowns of woven gold and with gold grounds, housings for the horses and palfreys of the same materials, and chains and jewels, that they are worth a vast amount of treasure; and some of the noblemen in this company, to do themselves honour, had spent as much as 200,000 crowns each."

Pasqualigo was at court when merchants from London came to honour Mary before she left for France. What he saw made an indelible mark on his memory:

"The Queen of France desired to see them all, and gave her hand to each of them. She wore a gown in the French fashion, of woven gold, very costly: She is very beautiful, and has not her match in all England. She is a young woman eighteen years old, tall, fair, and of a light complexion, with a colour, and most affable and graceful."

The jewel Mary wore suspended from her neck was one of the most splendid pieces the ambassador had ever seen:

"On her neck was a jewelled diamond, as large and as broad as a full sized finger, with a pear-shaped pearl beneath it, the size of a pigeon's egg, which jewel had been sent her as a present by the King of France . . . and the jewellers of 'the Row', whom the King desired to value it, estimated its worth at 60,000 crowns. It was marvellous that the existence of this diamond and pearl should never have been known; it was believed they had belonged to the late King of France, or to the Duke of Brittany, the father of the late Queen."[7]

Mary Tudor and her household set sail from England on 2 October 1514; on the lists of Mary's gentlewomen appointed to serve her in France was a reference to one "M. Boleyne".[8] For decades, historians wondered whether the *M* stood for the name "Mary" or a title such as "Mistress" or "Mademoiselle". The household list makes it clear that "Madamoyselle Boleyne" stayed in Mary Tudor's train after Louis XII sent the majority of her servants back to England. This may have been the same woman as "Marie Boulonne", the French version of the name of Anne Boleyn's sister, Mary, who figures on the list of Mary Tudor's attendants between October and December 1514.[9] Anne Boleyn's eminent biographer, the late Eric Ives, explained:

"In August 1514, therefore, Anne was on the list for France, but what happened then is not clear. Her sister, Mary, was also to go, and a list in the French archives shows that Mary Boleyn was one of the ladies in the household of the new Queen of France, but it makes no mention of Anne. The English sources concur. Mary Tudor left for France with a large escort and, after an appalling Channel crossing, arrived at Abbeville for the wedding, which took place on 9 October. The expectation was that the main party would then return to England, leaving a selected group to remain with Mary Tudor. This included one, and only one, Mistress Boleyn. In the event Louis XII refused to put up with the interference of some of the older women and sent them packing the day after the wedding, but among those retained was yet again a single 'Madmoyselle Boleyne'. The new queen stigmatised the survivors as 'such as never had experience nor knowledge how to advertise or give me counsel in any time of need', but these inexperienced young attendants evidently did not include Anne."[10]

Anne Boleyn was not in London to witness Mary Tudor setting sail to her new husband's land; she probably went to France directly from Margaret of Austria's court since her name does not appear on the list of women who accompanied Mary to France. Writing in 1536, Lancelot de Carle, a secretary to the French ambassador, wrote: "My lord, I am well aware that you know and have known for a long time that Anne Boullant first came from this country [England] when Mary [Tudor] left to go to join the King [Louis XII] in France to bring about the alliance of the two sovereigns."[11] William Camden, historian and antiquarian born in 1551, asserted that Anne "in her tender years was sent into France, and there waited first on Mary of England, wife to Lewis the Twelfth, and then on Claudia of Bretagne, wife of Francis I".[12] It was a new, exciting chapter in Anne's life, and one that would make an indelible mark on her character.

NOTES

[1] *Calendar of State Papers, Spain,* Volume 1, 1485-1509, n. 586.
[2] Erin A. Sadlack, *The French Queen's Letters*, p. 164.
[3] *The Manuscripts of J. Eliot Hodgkin*, p. 30.
[4] This will be further discussed in Chapter 4.
[5] Thomas Howard received the dukedom of Norfolk as a reward of his victory during the Battle of Flodden; the dukedom was conferred onto him on 1 February 1514.
[6] *Letters and Papers,* Volume 1, n. 3295.
[7] *Calendar of State Papers, Venice,* Volume 2, 1509-1519, n. 500.
[8] *Letters and Papers,* Volume 1, n. 5483.
[9] Eric Ives, *The Life and Death of Anne Boleyn*, p. 371.
Alison Weir, *Mary Boleyn: 'The Great and Infamous Whore'*, p. 74.
[10] Eric Ives, *The Life and Death of Anne Boleyn*, p. 371.
[11] Ibid., p. 27.
[12] William Camden, *The History of the Most Renowned and Victorious Princess Elizabeth*, p. 3.

Chapter 4:
Life at the French court

The country where Anne Boleyn would spend the next seven years was ruled by the Valois dynasty. King Louis XII, aged fifty-two, had been married twice but had no male heir. Louis's first wife was Joan of France, daughter of King Louis XI. Joan was deformed from birth, and her father fancied that the children born to Louis and Joan "will not cost them anything at all to support".[1] This effectively meant that Louis XI believed that Joan's infirmity would prevent her, as it truly did, from bearing children. Joan was said to have been "deformed and imperfect beyond what is normal with other women", but she would not accept that her royal marriage was invalid.[2] During the trial of annulment, Louis argued that his marriage to Joan was never consummated, but Joan denied this, saying that they had sex on many occasions. She also believed herself capable of bearing children despite never being pregnant during her marriage. The truth, as always, lay in the middle. Louis claimed that he tried to consummate his marriage to Joan, but every time he "wanted to have intercourse with her, he found a certain twistedness at the orifice of the vulva, such that his penis could not enter".[3]

Louis XII eventually won the annulment of his fruitless marriage and married Anne of Brittany, Charles VIII's widow. Anne was Duchess of Brittany in her own right, and the marriage agreement between her and her first husband stipulated that if Anne was widowed without having produced a son, the King's successor should marry her to keep the duchy of Brittany—a coveted prize—under French authority. Anne of Brittany is often known in history as "twice crowned Queen of France" since she was wife to two French kings.

As the years went by and Anne of Brittany produced no living sons, Louis XII was obliged to name an heir to satisfy his nobles. Louis's nearest kinsman in blood was Francis, son of Louise of Savoy and Charles, Count of Angoulême. Known as Francis of Angoulême, the boy was a popular figure throughout the country, and many believed he would become the next king. The fact that he was Louis XII's heir in the absence of a male heir produced by the royal couple caused tensions between Anne of Brittany and Francis's mother, Louise of Savoy. A son born to Louis XII and Anne of Brittany would deprive Louise of Savoy's boy of his royal inheritance, and for several long years Francis's right to the throne hung in the balance.

Anne, only eight months older than Louise, was in her early twenties when she became Queen of France for the second time, and it was reasonable to assume that she would be able to provide her husband with an heir to the throne. While married to Charles VIII, she had given birth to three sons successively, albeit only one, Charles Orland, lived past infancy, but he died at the age of three after contracting measles.[4] Louise followed Anne of Brittany's childbearing history, littered with miscarriages and stillbirths, with unabashed curiosity, detailing each pregnancy and its outcome in her journal. Anne's first child by Louis, Claude, was born in Louise's castle at Romorantin on 13 October 1499 at 8:54 p.m. With each of Anne of Brittany's failed pregnancies and dead infants, Louise's precious son's chances to inherit the crown became more and more real since the Salic law in France prevented women from assuming the crown.

Claude of France, as she was known in her country, would be an important personage in Anne Boleyn's life. From the moment of her birth in 1499 until 1510, when Anne of Brittany gave birth to another daughter, Claude was the only child in the royal nursery and, as the King's eldest daughter, the pivot of his matrimonial diplomacy. Although she had inherited a physical deformity from her mother—Anne was lame in one leg and used high-heeled shoes to disguise this infirmity—Claude was a desirable match, not only because she was the King's daughter but also because she stood to inherit the duchy of Brittany from her mother. Additionally, her dowry was comprised of the French claims to Asti, Milan, Genoa and Naples. In other words, Claude of France was one of the wealthiest heiresses of her day. Anne of Brittany planned to marry Claude to Charles, the future Holy Roman Emperor, because she wanted the duchy of Brittany to preserve its independence from France. Louis XII had other plans, however. In April 1500, when Claude was but four months old, her father swore a secret oath nullifying any marriage contracted by his daughter save only to Francis of Angoulême. This happened behind Anne of Brittany's back because she strongly opposed the match. The Queen opposed Claude's match to Francis because there was no love lost between Anne of Brittany and Francis's mother, Louise of Savoy. According to the sixteenth-century court historian Brantôme, the Queen "mortally hated Madame d'Angoulême" because their tempers were "quite unlike and not agreeing together".[5] The Queen also hated the thought that Francis was to become the next King because she believed that she was able to have more children herself.

Others seemed all too ready to accept that Anne of Brittany would never have a son, and in 1506 the Assembly of Notables pleaded with Louis XII for a marriage between Francis and Claude. Two years later, Louise proudly recorded that a marriage "de praesenti", wherein the couple verbally claimed each other in the present time, took place between Francis and Claude on 22 May 1507 in the palace of Plessis-lez-Tours. Over a year later, fourteen-year-old Francis was invited to take up permanent residence at court as Louis XII's heir presumptive. Although happy that her son was now formally recognised as the King's heir, Louise, somewhat bitterly, recorded in her journal that on 3 August 1508 "my son went away from Amboise to be a courtier and left me all alone".[6]

Although numerous pregnancies and miscarriages sapped her strength, Anne of Brittany never gave up. In 1508, after another miscarriage, the royal couple went on a pilgrimage to the church of St Maurice in Angers, a city famous for its flourishing cult of St René, patron of those seeking male offspring. On 29 October 1510, the Queen gave birth to another daughter, Renée, who—although slightly disfigured—lived past infancy and was a healthy and lively child. Two years later, the birth of a stillborn son spelled the end of Anne of Brittany's childbearing years and ensured the crown's passing to Louise of Savoy's son. This last pregnancy of the Queen's was, in hindsight, so important to Louise that she recorded it—with an outburst of discernible glee—in her journal:

"On 21 January, St Agnes's day, at Blois, Anne, Queen of France, had a son, but he could not impede the exaltation of my Caesar, for he lacked the breath of life. At that time I was at Amboise in my room, and the poor gentleman, who served my son and myself with such humble and loyal perseverance, brought me the news."[7]

Despite so many pregnancies, miscarriages and stillbirths, Anne of Brittany generally enjoyed good health, but this all changed in late 1513. She suffered from attacks of what one of her contemporaries called "gravel" and died on 9 January 1514 from a kidney stone, aged thirty-seven.[8] Almost immediately after Anne's death, rumours that Louis XII, "who had no sons", would remarry started to swirl at court and abroad.[9] To Louise and Francis, this new development potentially spelled disaster. When everyone learned that the King's intended bride was only eighteen years old, a wave of disbelief swept through France, but Louis was bent on remarrying and siring male heirs with his new wife.

With the death of Anne of Brittany, the last obstacle standing in the way of Francis of Angoulême's marriage to Claude of France disappeared and, it seemed, also paved the way towards Francis's kingship. The couple was married on 18 May 1514 while the court still mourned Anne of Brittany's death. Francis was confident that now, with Anne of Brittany dead and having the King's daughter as his wife, nothing could stand between himself and the crown. "Even if the King should commit the folly of marrying again", he was heard saying, "he will not live for long: any son he may have would be a child. This would necessitate regency, and in accordance with the constitution, the regent would be me".[10] This confidence was misplaced, however. The arrival of Mary Tudor, Louis's third wife, put a question mark over Francis's prospects of ever becoming king.

Mary Tudor was shocked when she first set her eyes on Louis XII. She was eighteen, beautiful and lively, while he, at fifty-two, was past his prime. Still, Mary understood that it was her duty to play the part of an obedient wife and greeted her husband with outward joy. She also understood that she had many enemies at her husband's court, Louise of Savoy chief amongst them. Afraid that a son borne by the young Queen would supersede her son, Francis, in the line of succession, Louise could hardly hide her contempt towards Mary. On 22 September 1514, she bitterly scribbled in her journal that Louis XII, "exceedingly old and weak", departed to Paris in order to greet his "young wife, Queen Mary".[11]

When Mary landed in France with her entourage, Louis arrived with his nobles to greet her. Marco Dandolo, the Venetian ambassador in France, recorded that:

"The King met her on the road, and kissed her; and then she entered the town, much honour being paid her. She came in excellent array; but in a storm on the passage one of her ships foundered, with ladies and others, and much plate and property was lost."[12]

Mary was clad in "very handsome stiff brocade" and travelled on a palfrey under a canopy of estate, accompanied by Francis of Angouleme. Antonio Triulzi, Bishop of Asti, wrote:

"Next came her litter, very beautiful, adorned with lilies; then five of the principal English ladies, very well dressed; then a carriage of brocade, on which were four ladies, followed by a second carriage with as many more ladies. Next came six ladies on horseback; and then a third carriage, of purple and crimson velvet, with four ladies; after which a crowd of ladies, some twenty in number; then 150 archers in three liveries. In this order they went to the Queen's house, which was near that of the King. It was a sumptuous entry, and these noblemen of England have very large chains, and are otherwise in good array."[13]

Anne Boleyn had probably reached France by this time to take part in her royal mistress's spectacular entry into Abbeville. The list of ladies who accompanied Mary Tudor in France still survives. Chief among them was "Dame Guildford", otherwise known as "Mother Guildford". Jane Guildford, née Vaux, was a seasoned lady-in-waiting. Born in 1469, she served as a maid of honour to Elizabeth of York and later as a lady-in-waiting to Margaret Beaufort and was present during Katharine of Aragon's marriage to Prince Arthur in St Paul's Cathedral in 1501. Jane was half-French; her mother, Katherine Vaux, née Peniston, was a daughter of an English exile living in Provence. Katherine served as a lady-in-waiting to Margaret of Anjou, wife of Henry VI, and followed her royal mistress to exile in 1476. She returned to England after Margaret died in 1482; she appeared as one of Elizabeth of York's ladies as "Dame Katheryn Vaux" during the Queen's coronation in 1487.

Following in her mother's footsteps, Jane showed fierce loyalty to the royal women she served. She first became lady governess to Henry VII's daughters, Margaret and Mary, and impressed the scholar Erasmus, who visited the royal nursery at Eltham Palace in 1497.

Jane Guildford, much beloved by Mary Tudor, supervised other ladies-in-waiting and maids of honour. Other ladies of high rank who served Mary in France included Agnes Howard, Duchess of Norfolk, and her daughter Anne de Vere, Countess of Oxford. There was also Margaret Grey, Marchioness of Dorset; Elizabeth Stanley, Baroness Monteagle; and Florence Grey, Baroness Grey de Wilton. There were also other ladies including Elizabeth Grey, sister of Thomas Grey, second Marquis of Dorset. She was related to Mary since they were both granddaughters of Elizabeth Woodville. Two more ladies, Elizabeth Ferrers and Anne Devereux, served in Mary's Privy Chamber. Alice Denys, Anne Jerningham, "M. Wotton" and "M. Boleyne" served as chamberers.[14] As noted in the previous chapter, the "M. Boleyne" may have been Mary Boleyn, Anne's sister, or an abbreviation for "mistress".

Mary Tudor married Louis XII on 9 October 1514. A tapestry depicting the royal marriage was later ordered from Tournai. Nine women accompanied Mary in this tapestry, and it is widely believed that Anne Boleyn was among them. "The Queen was dressed in a gown of stiff gold brocade, her headgear being in the English fashion, and she wore jewels of very great price", observed the Venetian ambassador. "Then came the English princesses and noble ladies, in number 24, wearing in like manner many jewels on their heads, and garments of gold brocade, so that never was such pomp witnessed", he added further.[15] Louise of Savoy sourly observed in her journal that it was an "amorous wedding" that took place in the morning, and in the evening the royal couple "went to bed together". This is confirmed by the Venetian ambassador, who reported that "in the evening, Madame [Claude] the King's daughter, wife of Monseigneur d'Angoulême, went to visit her [Mary], and they gave a ball". The whole court was "banqueting, dancing and making good cheer", and later that evening "the Queen was taken away from the entertainment by Madame [Claude] to go and sleep with the King."[16] The next morning, Louis XII emerged from his bedchamber and boasted that "thrice last night did he cross the river and would have done more had he so desired." "Crossing the river" was a subtle allusion to consummating his marriage to Mary, who discreetly remained silent on the subject.[17] Another contemporary observer, Robert de la Marck, seigneur de Fleuranges, reported that the King "claimed that he had done marvels" in his bedchamber.[18]

Mary's stepdaughter, Claude, was only three years younger than the new Queen. Everyone praised Mary's beauty and charm, and Claude felt jealous and betrayed by her father. According to Robert de la Marck, Claude "was greatly distressed, for her mother had been dead only a short while, and now she was obliged to serve her [Mary Tudor] as she had formerly served the Queen her mother".[19] Claude had shared an exceptionally close relationship with her late mother. Although, as a royal princess, she was looked after by an array of governesses from her early childhood, Anne of Brittany had taken a keen interest in her daughter's upbringing and exchanged letters with her on a regular basis. Her mother's death was a huge blow for Claude, who was now left with few friends.

Anne of Brittany had entrusted both of her daughters to the care of the woman she never loved, Louise of Savoy, knowing that as her eldest child's prospective mother-in-law, Louise was the best choice as a guardian and mentor. A somewhat exculpatory entry in Louise's journal reveals how she felt about this task. She fulfilled it honourably, she claimed. "Everyone knows it", Louise insisted, "truth recognises it; experience proves it; moreover, common report proclaims it".[20] Other sources, however, claimed that Louise was abusive towards Claude. Brantôme, for instance, wrote that Louise "treated her harshly".[21] Anne Boleyn pitied the young princess, who was approximately the same age as she. They were different in appearance; Anne had a swarthy complexion, dark eyes and hair and was slender and tall whereas Claude was pale, small and plump and had deformed hips. Yet they shared interests in music and poetry, and, thanks to Anne's talent for languages, could talk in Claude's native language. An unlikely friendship formed between the two, and Claude would later take Anne into her own household.

As was customary, Louis XII planned to send most of his new wife's servants back to England. He was becoming tired of Mary's servants. He was especially tired of Mother Guildford's constant meddling into his private affairs. The forty-five-year-old Lady Guildford was very protective of Queen Mary, and the two were often in each other's company, Mary confiding in Lady Guildford and seeking her advice on marital life. The morning following her wedding, Louis XII discharged his wife's English household. Outraged, Mary penned a letter to her brother, writing:

"My good Brother, as heartily as I can I recommend me unto your Grace, marvelling much that I never heard from you since our departing, so often as I have sent and written unto you. And now am I left post alone in effect, for on the morn after marriage my chamberlain and all other men servants were discharged, and in likewise my mother Guildford with other my women and maidens, except such as never had experience nor knowledge how to advertise or give me counsel in any time of need, which is to be feared more shortly than your Grace thought at the time of my departing, as my mother Guildford can more plainly show your Grace than I can write, to whom I beseech you to give credence. And if it may be by any mean possible I humbly require you to cause my said mother Guildford to repair hither once again. For else if any chance hap other than weal I shall not know where nor by whom to ask any good counsel to your pleasure nor yet to mine own profit. I marvel much that my lord of Norfolk would at all times so lightly grant everything at their requests here. I am well assured that when ye know the truth of everything as my mother Guildford can show you, ye would full little have thought I should have been thus treated; that would God my lord of York [Thomas Wolsey] had come with me in the room of Norfolk; for then I am sure I should have been left much more at my heartsease than I am now. And thus I bid your Grace farewell with [mutilated] as ever had Prince: and more heartsease than I have now.

[I beseech] give credence to my mother Guildford.

By your loving sister,

MARY, Queen of France."[22]

Mary's dependence on Lady Guildford was clear from this letter. "I have not yet seen in France any lady or gentlewoman so necessary for me as she is, nor yet so meet [suitable] to do the King my brother service as she is", she wrote in a letter to Thomas Wolsey, Archbishop of York.[23] Mary's letter reveals that she felt ill at ease at the French court, surrounded by hostile courtiers and people who made fun of her youth, implying that she would carry the King to his grave. Mary cloaked her true feelings towards Louis XII with a display of wifely obedience, but deep down she was disgusted with this old, decrepit man who was racked by gout. Thomas Wolsey took pity on Mary and wrote to the French King, praising Lady Guildford and begging him to approve of her return to Mary's household:

"Since the King, my sovereign lord and master, your good brother had ordered on account of the true, perfect, and entire confidence which he had in Mistress Guildford that she should be with the Queen, his sister, your wife, on account of the good manners and experience which he knew her to have, and also because she speaks the language well: in order also that the said Queen, his sister, might be better advised, and taught by her how she ought to conduct herself towards you under all circumstances, considering, moreover, that the Queen, his said good sister, is a young lady and that she should be abroad, not understanding the language perfectly, and having no acquaintance with any of the ladies there, to whom she might disclose such feelings as women are given to, and that she had no one of her acquaintance to whom she could familiarly tell and disclose her mind, that she might find herself desolate as it were, and might thereby entertain regret and displeasure, which peradventure might cause her to have some sickness and her bodily health to be impaired, which God forbid, and should such an accident happen, I believe, Sir, that you would be most grieved and displeased."[24]

Lady Guildford was still at Boulogne, hoping to be recalled to Mary's side, but Louis XII had no intention of reappointing her. He informed the English ambassador that "his wife and he be in good and perfect love as ever two creatures can be, and both of age to rule themselves, and not to have servants that should look to rule him or her". Ever since their arrival, Lady Guildford "began to take upon her not only to rule the Queen but also that she should not come to him but that she should be with her, nor that no lady nor lord should speak with her but she should hear it, and began to set a murmur and a banding among the ladies of the court". It was a custom in France for matronly ladies to supervise their charges at all times, and Lady Guildford appeared to have stayed with Mary even when Louis came to her chamber to be "merry" with her, i.e. to have sex with her. He told the English envoy that he had a "sickly body and not at all times that he would be merry with his wife to have any strange [foreign] woman with her, but one that he is well-acquainted withal, before whom he durst be merry".[25] Lady Guildford was not recalled, and Mary soon realised that not having her imposing presence at all times proved beneficial. Mary "loved my Lady Guildford well, but she is content that she cometh not, for she is in that case that she may well be without her, for she may do what she will".[26]

Among the ladies who stayed with Queen Mary in France was "Mademoiselle Boleyne", accompanied by Elizabeth Grey, Mary Fiennes, Elizabeth Grey of Wilton, Anne Jerningham and Jeanne Barnesse.[27] Anne and the other maidens couldn't help but notice that the French King's health was deteriorating. On 13 October 1514, the English ambassadors in France wrote to Henry VIII that Louis XII suffered from a renewed attack of gout and was confined to his bed. Mary, they assured, "was continually with him, of whom he made as much as she reported to us herself, as it is possible for any man to make of a lady".[28]

Indeed, Louis was very generous towards Mary. Although he upset her by dismissing her attendants, he found means of consoling her. The English ambassadors reported that each day Louis gave Mary expensive jewels, including "a ruby two inches and a half long, and as big as a man's finger, hanging by two chains of gold at every end" and "a great diamond tablet with a great round pearl hanging by it". But this was not everything. Every day, they wrote, Louis presented Mary with "rings with stones of great estimation".[29] Although hurt by the fact that her favoured attendants had been dismissed, Mary reciprocated with displays of wifely obedience and affection.

When Charles Brandon, Duke of Suffolk, one of the English envoys, was invited to an audience with the royal couple, he saw the bedridden Louis XII "and the Queen sitting by his bedside".[30] When the King's health improved, he was able to confirm that his new wife was to be crowned and anointed without any further delay. Mary was crowned on 5 November 1514 at the Basilica of St Denis. Anne Boleyn had never seen a coronation before, and what she saw that day dazzled her. Francis of Angoulême led Mary to the choir on the right side of the high altar, where she was to be anointed. The English ambassadors related:

"And first the Queen's Grace knelt before the altar in a place prepared therefore, and there the said Cardinal of Pree anointed her, and after delivered her the sceptre in her right hand, and the verge of the hand of Justice in her left hand; and after that he put a ring upon her finger, and fourthly he set the crown on her head, which done, the said Duke of Brittany [Francis] led her up a stage made on the left side of the altar, directly before us, where she was set in a chair under a throne, and the said Duke stood behind her holding the crown from her head to ease her of the weight thereof; and then began the high Mass sung by the said Cardinal, whereat the Queen offered, and after Agnus Dei she received the sacrament and, Mass done, she departed to Palace, and we to our lodgings to our dinners."[31]

On 7 November 1514, Mary entered Paris as Queen of France, accompanied by her ladies-in-waiting. Mary was not yet fluent in French, and she used the help of translators to understand the meaning of the pageants celebrating her as France's new consort. Mary's spectacular wedding, her coronation and entry to Paris were the highlights of her brief queenship. These events were also to be the first and the last grand events she would experience as Queen of France. Although Louis XII boasted of his success in the marital bed, the King's health started to deteriorate soon after his wedding. He changed his unruffled lifestyle for Mary, who enjoyed pastimes such as dancing and hunting. Contemporary observers condemned her youth and blamed her for exerting ruinous influence on her husband's health. Mary Tudor's beauty and stamina fascinated her aging husband, who was very eager to please her and keep up with her. Robert de la Marck wrote about a malicious pamphlet circulating in France at the time, according to which the King of England had sent the King of France a young filly to gallop him off to hell or to heaven.[32]

According to Robert de la Marck, seigneur de Fleuranges, during the winter of 1514, Louis XII "took lodgings at Tournelles in Paris because it had the best climate, and also he did not feel very strong, because he had desired to be a pleasing companion with his wife; but he deceived himself, as he was not the man for it . . . inasmuch as he had for a long time been very sick, particularly with gout, and for five or six years he had thought that he would die of it . . . because he was given up by the doctors, and he lived on a very strict diet which he broke when he was with his wife; and the doctors told him that if he continued, he would die from his pleasure".[33]

Indeed, Louis "died of his pleasure" on 1 January 1515. According to the English chronicler Raphael Holinshed, the King "so fervently loved Mary that he gave himself over to behold too much her excellent beauty bearing then eighteen years of age, nothing considering the proportion of his own years, nor his decayed complexion; so that he fell into the rage of fever, which drawing to it a sudden flux, overcame in one instant his life".[34] After eighty-two days of being Queen of France, Mary Tudor was now a widow. Louis XII's death meant that Louise of Savoy's golden boy, Francis, was now King, but there was one last issue to resolve before he could put a crown on his head. Etiquette required that a dowager Queen retired from public view for one month after her royal husband's death. The most important reason behind this custom was determining whether the Queen was pregnant. Should she prove to be with child, there would be no King until the birth.

Mary Tudor now became "la Reine Blanche", or "the White Queen", wearing white mourning gowns and retiring to a darkened chamber lit only by candlelight in the Hôtel de Cluny. At the Hôtel de Cluny, the young widow was allowed to receive guests. Francis of Angoulême "visited her often" and acted with "all possible kindness" towards her.[35] The Venetian ambassador reported that Francis "went every day to visit the Queen Dowager, who was sorrowful, lamenting much the death of her husband".[36] Three weeks into her confinement, Francis broached the delicate matter of the Queen's pregnancy and asked Mary directly "if he could consider himself King because he knew not whether she was pregnant or not." Mary answered that "he might and that she knew of no other King than he, for she had no idea of having any offspring that could prevent".[37] Francis was thus proclaimed King.

As a royal widow, Mary Tudor was once again swiftly pushed into the marriage market. At nineteen, she was young and "the most attractive and beautiful woman ever seen".[38] Whoever controlled her—in this case it was Francis I, the new King of France—could use her for his political advantage. Thomas Wolsey, the Archbishop of York and Henry VIII's closest adviser, was very well aware of this fact when he wrote to the Dowager Queen Mary that "if any motion of marriage or other thing fortune to be made unto you, in no wise give hearing to the same". Mary's reply was courteous but assertive. She thanked the well-willing Wolsey for his "good lessons" but objected to his lack of confidence in her own judgment: "My Lord, I trust the King, my brother, and you will not reckon in me such childhood." She was not naïve, and she had already decided that she would not become any man's pawn this time around. In fact, she was well aware that Henry VIII and Wolsey, although two friendly souls, underestimated her potential. She informed them both that she would marry "where my mind is". Henry VIII knew very well what that entailed, and Mary did not hesitate to remind her brother about a promise he made her before she left for France three months earlier. Always the realist, Mary was aware that sooner or later the sickly French King would die and she would become a widow. She already had plans for her prospective widowhood, and, to make sure that her plans would come true, she extracted a promise from her brother:

"Sir, I beseech Your Grace that you will keep all the promises that you promised me when I took my leave of you by the waterside. Sir, Your Grace knoweth well that I did marry for your pleasure at this time, and now I trust you will suffer me to marry as me liketh for to do . . .

wherefore I beseech Your Grace to be a good Lord and brother unto me."[39]

In the same letter, Mary threatened that if she would be pressured to marry for political reasons again, she would rather join a nunnery than relent. The young Queen Dowager surely did not entertain any such thought; she was way too pretty and lively to waste away in a convent, and she knew it. She only hoped that her brother would prove to be the chivalrous King he always styled himself to be and honour his promises. A convent, she knew, was not an option because "I think Your Grace would be very sorry . . . and all your realm", but it was a nice way of showing her elder brother how determined she was to get what she wanted, and she wanted Charles Brandon.[40]

Henry knew that his younger sister was in love with Charles Brandon, his boon companion, friend and the man he had created the Duke of Suffolk only recently and against murmurs at court. Charles Brandon's family was staunchly devoted to the Tudors; his own father, William, was killed while holding Henry VII's banner at the Battle of Bosworth in 1485. Raised at court, Charles Brandon became Henry VIII's constant companion, confidante and close friend. They enjoyed the same pastimes and excelled in them, and both loved women and surrounded themselves with the same friends. Brandon was not only "a very handsome man" but also "one of the chief noblemen of England".[41] Even foreign dignitaries were aware that Brandon was like "a second King", and his graces were well worth cultivating because "it is he who does and undoes".[42] Wherever Henry went, Brandon was right by his side. No wonder, then, that the King's younger sister fell in love with this energetic man some twelve years her senior, who was always present in her life, and now wanted to become his wife.

Anne Boleyn knew Charles Brandon and his daughter, also named Anne. At some unknown date, perhaps around the time of the meeting between the Hapsburgs and Tudors in Lille in the autumn of 1513, Charles Brandon's daughter was selected as Margaret of Austria's maid of honour. During that meeting, Charles snatched a ring from Margaret's finger, which was a custom in England and indicated romantic courtship, and fuelled rumours that Margaret would marry him. Margaret playfully called Brandon a "thief" in her native language and then in Flemish, but Brandon didn't understand and took the ring with him. Margaret was confused and later she had to deny the rumours that she planned to marry Brandon. If Anne Brandon joined the archduchess's court when Anne

Boleyn was still there, the two girls certainly met. Anne Brandon stayed in the Netherlands longer than Anne Boleyn, however, returning home in the summer of 1515.

What Anne thought about Brandon's "foolish behaviour" with Margaret of Austria remains unknown, but she may have felt contempt for him. The two certainly didn't get along later in their lives.[43] Whether Anne and Mary Tudor were aware that Charles was not free to remarry is another matter. Charles's marital history was littered with discarded brides and children of dubious legitimacy. He first pre-contracted himself to Anne Browne, with whom he had a daughter. If consummated, pre-contract was as binding as marriage but should have been followed by a formal church ceremony. Brandon, however, discarded Anne Browne and went on to marry her aunt, Margaret Neville, a wealthy widow in her early forties. This, no doubt, was a marriage of convenience for Brandon, who was some twenty years younger than his new bride. "In this country, young men marry old ladies", wrote the Venetian ambassador, Sebastiano Giustiniani, pointing out that "here, for instance, is the Duke of Suffolk, who at nineteen married a lady for her wealth . . . old enough to be his mother".[44]

What happened next is not entirely clear. The only certainty is that Brandon decided to discard Margaret Neville. One source says that he had obtained a divorce from her, citing his consummated pre-contract with Anne Browne, whereas another claims that there was no pre-contract with Anne Browne when he married Lady Neville, and thus no legal ground for the divorce existed. In any case, Brandon promptly returned to Anne Browne and had one more daughter by her before she died in 1510. Motivated by financial profit yet again, Brandon soon became engaged to his ward, Elizabeth Grey, Viscountess Lisle, but there never was a marriage contracted between the two due to Elizabeth's tender age.

When Brandon had his first audience with Francis on 3 February 1515, after arriving at the head of the English embassy to France, Francis greeted him with these words: "My Lord of Suffolk, so it is that there is a bruit in this my realm, that you are come to marry with the Queen, your Master's sister". At first, Brandon tried to deny this, writing to Wolsey:

"I answered and said that I trusted His Grace would not reckon so great a folly in me, to come into a strange realm and to marry a Queen of the realm, without his knowledge, and without authority from the King my master to him, and that they both might be content."[45]

Francis stopped teasing Brandon when he told him that Mary had revealed "her heart's desire" to him and used a certain password that only Mary could have known. Francis assured the surprised Brandon that "I shall never fail unto you, but to help and advance this matter betwixt her and you, with as good will as I would for mine own self".[46] Brandon was clearly overwhelmed by the speed of events and begged Wolsey to send him his precious advice. Wolsey wrote back immediately, declaring that he had shown the contents of his letter to Henry VIII, who appeared to have been perfectly happy with the way Charles Brandon handled the conversation with Francis I.

On 4 February 1515, Charles headed to meet the Dowager Queen Mary at the Hôtel de Cluny. She was distraught, and, crying incessantly, she told Charles that if he would not marry her within four days, she would never be his. The reason why she was so distraught was that two English friars had visited her and told her that if she returned to England unwed, the King's council would never allow her to marry Charles Brandon. Fearing that the friars were sent by someone of Henry VIII's Privy Council to warn her, she decided to constrain Brandon "to break such promises as he made Your Grace". She had also heard from various French nobles that her brother planned to marry her off to Charles of Castile, and she would "rather be torn to pieces" than go to Flanders.[47] She warned Brandon that if he refused to marry her immediately, he would lose her forever because she would not return to England with him.

Was Anne Boleyn still in Mary Tudor's household when this drama was unfolding? It seems that she was. According to Lancelot de Carle, who wrote about Anne in a biographical poem in 1536, Claude appointed Anne as her maid of honour after Mary Tudor left France—and this didn't happen until April 1515. This means that Anne witnessed Mary Tudor's relations with Charles Brandon firsthand. "I never saw a woman so weep", Brandon wrote to Henry VIII. Indeed, Mary was hysterical and forced Brandon to marry her at once, without consent of Francis I and Henry VIII. On 5 March 1515, Brandon wrote to Wolsey:

"My Lord, so it is that when I came to Paris, I heard many things which put me in great fear, and so did the Queen both; and the Queen would never let me be in rest till I had granted her to be married. And so to be plain with you, I have married her heartily and have lain with her, insomuch that I fear me lest she be with child."[48]

It now dawned on the couple that Mary might be pregnant and they should have a second, public wedding before their journey to England. "My Lord", Brandon implored Wolsey, "at the reverence of God help that I may be married as I go out of France, openly, for many things of which I will advertise [inform] you by mine next letters. Give me your advice whether the French King and his mother shall write again to the King for this open marriage; seeing that this privy marriage is done, and that I think none otherwise but that she is with child".[49] Whether Mary was mistaken about her condition, suffered a miscarriage or purposely misled Charles will never be known for sure. The couple's first child, Henry, was not born until 1516.

According to Robert de la Marck, Francis I was not happy about this secret marriage and burst into a rage when he learned about it. "I did not think you had been so base", he confronted Brandon, "and if I chose to do my duty, I should, this very hour, have your head taken off your shoulders".[50] The reason behind Francis I's rage is obvious. When he agreed to intercede with Henry VIII on their behalf, the French King thought about the future and did not expect that Mary and Charles would be so bold as to break the etiquette that required a royal widow to wait at least a year before she contracted a new marriage. The unseemly haste felt like an assault on the memory of Louis XII. Mary, on the other hand, had a different story to tell. She informed Francis about her love for Charles Brandon not because she needed his assistance, but because she was "in extreme pain and annoyance" caused by "such suit as the French King made unto me, not according with mine own honour". So she told him everything because she feared that if she would keep this from his knowledge, he would not treat Brandon well and would renew his "former malfantasy and suits".[51]

Whether Francis truly molested Mary with importunate insinuations will never be known for a fact, but several decades later, courtly gossip had it that Francis had been in love with Mary and eager to consummate that love with her. Some clue to Francis I's feelings about Mary is found in a little acidic comment he inscribed on a sketch of the Dowager Queen in the Album d'Aix: "Pleus sale que royne." This phrase is usually translated into English as "more dirty than queenly". In 1863, the French scholar Étienne Antoine Benoit Rouard pointed out that it is difficult to unequivocally interpret this phrase and offered another version rendered into modern French as "Plus folle que royne" because an *S* resembles an *F* in Francis I's handwriting. It could be thus translated into English as "More foolish than queenly" or, alternatively, "More fool than a Queen".[52] Despite this opinion, Francis agreed to a public wedding ceremony and appeared as a guest of honour. His mother, with thinly veiled scorn, recorded in her journal that on "Saturday the last day of March, the Duke of Suffolk, a person of low estate whom Henry VIII had sent as ambassador to the King, married Mary of England".[53]

Attending this wedding was probably Anne Boleyn's last duty as Mary Tudor's maid of honour. Mary, Charles and their servants left France on 16 April 1515. Mary argued that as former Queen of France she had the right to retain jewels and plate she received from the late Louis XII, but Francis I argued that these were crown jewels that belonged to current Queen consort—his wife, Claude. Mary shipped some of the jewels off to England, enraging Francis, who gave her only four paltry rings as a parting gift. Francis was still displeased that Mary had sent a large diamond known as "the Mirror of Naples" to Henry VIII. This had been the most valuable piece in the French collection.[54]

Mary and Charles reached England on 2 May 1515 and were officially married at Greenwich Palace on 13 May—it was their third wedding ceremony. Anne Boleyn was not in their entourage. "After Mary returned to this country", wrote Lancelot de Carle many years later, Anne "was kept back by Claude, who succeeded as Queen".[55] The fact that Anne was able to stay at the French court despite the scandal caused by her previous royal mistress speaks volumes about Anne's character. Margaret of Austria was probably right when she wrote that Anne was exceedingly "bright and pleasant for her young age". Queen Claude shared this view.

But there is also another, alternative version of Anne's stay in France. According to this version, Anne lived in the small town of Briis-sous-Forges in northern France.

NOTES

[1] D. L. d'Avray, *Dissolving Royal Marriages: A Documentary History, 860–1600*, p. 215.
[2] Ibid., p. 203.
[3] Ibid., p. 215.
[4] Philip de Commines, *The Memoirs of Philip de Commines*, Volume 2, p. 112
[5] Pierre de Bourdeille, seigneur de Brantôme, *The Book of the Ladies*, p. 39.
[6] *Journal de Louise de Savoie*, p. 87.
[7] Ibid.

[8] Robert III de La Marck, seigneur de Fleuranges, *Mémoires du maréchal de Florange, dit le Jeune Adventureaux*, Volume 1, p. 147.
[9] *Calendar of State Papers Relating To English Affairs in the Archives of Venice,* Volume 2, n. 367.
[10] R.J.Knecht, *Francis I*, p. 10.
[11] *Journal de Louise de Savoie*, p. 89.
[12] *Calendar of State Papers, Venice,* Volume 2, n. 507.
[13] Ibid., n. 508.
[14] John Leland, *De Rebus Brittanicis Collectanea*, Volume 2, p. 703.
[15] *Calendar of State Papers, Venice,* Volume 2, n. 510.
[16] Ibid, n. 507.
[17] Ibid., n. 511.
[18] Erin A. Sadlack, *The French Queen's Letters*, p. 70.
[19] Robert III de La Marck, seigneur de Fleuranges, *Mémoires du maréchal de Florange, dit le Jeune Adventureaux*, Volume 1, p. 158.
[20] *Journal de Louise de Savoie*, p. 89.
[21] Pierre de Bourdeille, seigneur de Brantôme, *The Book of the Ladies*, p. 219.
[22] Mary Croom Brown, *Mary Tudor Queen of France*, p. 122, 123.
[23] Ibid., p. 124.
[24] Ibid., p. 125.
[25] *The Westminster Review*, Volume 3, April-July 1827, p. 144.
[26] Mary Croom Brown, *Mary Tudor Queen of France*, p. 127.
[27] Letters and Papers, Volume 1, n. 3357.
[28] Henry Ellis, *Original Letters Illustrative of English History,* 2nd series, Volume 1, pp. 240-241.
[29] Ibid.
[30] Ibid.
[31] Henry Ellis, *Original Letters Illustrative of English History, 2nd series*, Volume 1, p. 250-258.
[32] Erin A. Sadlack, *The French Queen's Letters*, p. 74.
[33] Walter C. Richardson, *Mary Tudor*, p. 125.
[34] Raphael Holinshed, *Holinshed's Chronicles of England, Scotland and Ireland*, Volume 3, p. 610.
[35] Erin A. Sadlack, *The French Queen's Letters*, p. 93.
[36] *Calendar of State Papers, Venice,* Volume 2, 1509-1519, n. 573, 574.
[37] Mary Anne Everett Green, *Lives of the Princesses of England: From the Norman Conquest,* Volume 5, p. 78.
[38] *Calendar of State Papers Relating To English Affairs in the Archives of Venice,* Volume 2, 1509-1519, n. 600.

[39] Mary Anne Everett Wood, *Letters of Royal and Illustrious Ladies of Great Britain*, Volume 1, p. 188.
[40] Ibid.
[41] *Calendar of State Papers Relating To English Affairs in the Archives of Venice*, Volume 2, 1509-1519, n. 464.
[42] *Letters and Papers, Foreign and Domestic, Henry VIII*, Volume 1, 1509-1514, n. 2171.
[43] Eric Ives, *The Life and Death of Anne Boleyn*, p. 28.
[44] Walter C. Richardson, *Mary Tudor*, p. 164.
[45] Mary Anne Everett Wood, *Letters of Royal and Illustrious Ladies of Great Britain*, Volume 1, p. 195.
[46] Ibid., p. 196.
[47] Ibid., pp. 200-201.
[48] *Letters and Papers, Foreign and Domestic, Henry VIII*, Volume 2, 1515-1518, n. 224.
[49] Walter C. Richardson, *Mary Tudor*, p. 173.
[50] Mary Anne Everett Green, *Lives of the Princesses of England: From the Norman Conquest*, Volume 5, p. 90.
[51] Ibid., p. 86.
[52] Étienne Antoine Benoit Rouard, *François Ier chez Mme De Boisy*, p. 34.
[53] *Journal de Louise de Savoie*, p. 89.
[54] *Letters and Papers, Foreign and Domestic, Henry VIII*, Volume 2, 1515-1518, n. 343.
[55] Susan Walters Schmid, *Anne Boleyn, Lancelot de Carle, and the Uses of Documentary Evidence*, p. 112.

Chapter 5:
The legend of Briis-sous-Forges

When Francis I assumed the throne in January 1515, he was twenty-one years old. The English chronicler Raphael Holinshed captured the feeling of high expectations surrounding Francis's accession:

"The world had such a hope in his virtues, and such an opinion of his magnanimity and such a concept of his judgment and wit, that everyone confessed that of very long time there was none raised up to the crown with a greater expectation. He was made the more agreeable to the fancies of men by the consideration of his age, bearing then but two and twenty years; his excellent features and proportion of body, by his great liberality, and general humanity, together with the ripe knowledge he had in many things. But especially he pleased greatly the nobility, to whom he transferred many singular and great favours."

As Holinshed explained, Francis "was preferred to the succession of the kingdom before the daughters [Claude and Renée] of the dead King by virtue and disposition of the

Salic law, a law very ancient in the realm of France, which excluded from the royal dignity all women".[1] Claude's thoughts touching the preferment of her husband's claim over hers are not recorded, but we may assume that she was content with the role of a royal consort because she had been groomed to become one from her early childhood. At the same time, she was well aware of her importance and the political implications of her marriage to Francis. Despite being Queen of France, Claude was simultaneously Duchess of Brittany in her own right and sought to assume her own independent political role as such.

The fifteen-year-old Queen was very popular in France. She was widely praised for her pious demeanour and sense of duty. Although she displayed wifely obedience, she may have been apprehensive about her marriage to Francis. Despite her physical shortcomings, Claude was a grand matrimonial prize, and Francis sealed his position as heir to the throne by marrying her. Yet Claude's mother was always against the match, and it is possible that she raised Claude with deep distrust, or perhaps even hatred, of Francis and his mother. "If Queen Anne had lived, never would have Madame Claude have been married to King François for she foresaw the evil treatment she was certain to receive", Brantôme wrote with the benefit of hindsight years later.[2] Claude's wedding, four months after her beloved mother's death, was a sad, sombre affair, with the young couple dressed in mourning. Francis disrespected his wife, leaving her company to pursue new amours—something he would do countless times during their marriage.

Claude knew that despite her importance as Louis XII's daughter, she must prove her worth by giving birth to a male heir, a duty her mother never fulfilled. The importance of becoming the mother of a son was emphasised in the epitaph composed to honour Anne of Brittany after her death: "I married King Louis XII, wearing the crown of the French, with whom I had only two daughters."[3] Claude knew that being wife of the King meant nothing as long as she was not the mother of his sons; her own father had repudiated his first barren and deformed wife to marry Claude's mother, and the pope made no qualms about helping him do it. Luckily for Claude, she was pregnant when Francis became King.

One of the early descriptions of Claude was recorded by Mercurino di Gattinara, the Italian statesman who had an audience with her on 15 February 1515. Gattinara reported to Margaret of Austria that Claude's face resembled that of her late mother, Anne of Brittany. She was also "very small and strangely corpulent" and, he added to emphasize her pregnancy, "already very big".[4] Gattinara expressed his concern about Claude's delivery, pointing out that she would have problems bringing forth the child if it was as strong as its father, Francis I. Like her mother, Claude suffered from certain malformations that gave rise to fears about her childbearing capabilities. She was "small in stature, plain and badly lame in both hips" but was said to be "very cultivated, generous and pious".[5]

Claude was often criticised for her frail physique. Prior to her wedding to Francis, Pierre de Rohan, Marshal of Gié, told Louise of Savoy that he would rather see her son "married to a simple shepherdess of this kingdom than to Madame Claude because the misfortune is such that Madame Claude is deformed in body and unable to bear children".[6] When she became pregnant in late 1514, most people assumed that Claude would die in childbirth. According to one English observer, rumour had it that even the pope alleged that "the French asserted the present Queen would die in childbed".[7] In May 1515 Venetian ambassador saw her and although he praised her clothes because she was wearing soprarizzo velvet, a rare fabric woven in Venice, he was not impressed with her appearance, describing her as "short of stature, dark, lame in both legs, very ugly".[8] He also recorded that she was five months pregnant. It is interesting to note that the Italian ambassadors used the same word to describe Claude, "brutissima" (very ugly) as they did to describe her father's first wife, Joan of Valois. Claude eventually proved her critics wrong, giving birth to seven healthy children during the period of 1515 to 1524. Historian Simone Bertière calculated that Claude was pregnant 63 of the 122 months of her reign.[9] These frequent pregnancies took their toll on the Queen's fragile health, and she could not attend her husband's court and play a ceremonial role as often as etiquette required.

When she established her household, Claude followed her late mother's example. Anne of Brittany was, according to the testimony of Brantôme, "the first Queen to hold a great Court of ladies".[10] "Her suite was very large of ladies and young girls, for she refused none", he relates, "she even enquired of the noblemen of her Court whether they had daughters, and what they were, and asked to have them brought to her". Just like Anne of Beaujeu's court, Anne of Brittany's establishment "was a noble school for ladies; she had them taught and brought up wisely; and all, taking pattern by her, made themselves wise and virtuous".[11] In 1498, a total number of 253 servants peopled Anne of Brittany's household; by 1523, Claude had 285 servants, which means that she not only maintained but even surpassed the high standards set by her beloved mother.[12]

Although it is sometimes suggested that Claude's court was "run almost as a convent", there is no evidence to that effect.[13] Quite the contrary; Claude enjoyed reading romances and had a deep appreciation for poetry. Amongst her ladies-in-waiting was Anne de Graville, the sole female French court poet of that period and a strong-minded individual who married her husband, Pierre de Balsac, against her father's wishes and eloped with him.[14] Claude requested poems and translations of Latin texts from Anne; *La Belle Dame sans Mercy* (*The Beautiful Lady without Mercy*), a re-adaptation of Alain Chartier's poem, and a historical romance, *Palamon and Arcita.* Both were dedicated to Queen Claude, whom Anne de Graville extolled beyond measure as her patroness.[15]

Francis I was known as a notorious lover of female charms from the early years of his reign. One contemporary observed that he was "a great womaniser", and many other dignitaries commented upon his "whoring", while Henry VIII heard that Francis was "not much attached to his

Queen".[16] Yet Brantôme recorded that Claude was "much beloved by her husband" and an eyewitness who travelled through France concluded that "it is a matter of common report that he holds his wife the Queen in such honour and respect that when in France and with her he has never failed to sleep with her each night".[17] It appears that Claude never raised any objection to Francis's extramarital affairs, even though some of them humiliated her. When he was still a dauphin, Francis fell passionately in love with Mary Tudor and, if we believe Mary's complaints, he tried to bed her but was thwarted. Unable to entice Mary Tudor into his bed, Francis moved on to court other women. According to the prevailing opinion among historians, he took Mary Boleyn, Anne's sister, as his mistress, later boasting that he "knew her here in France 'per una grandissima ribalda et infame sopre tutte'. The phrase "una grandissima ribalda et infame sopre tutte" does not have one coherent translation into English, and there are several versions of it proposed by historians. According to Eric Ives, the phrase translates as "a great wanton and notoriously infamous", while Mary Boleyn's biographer, Josephine Wilkinson, translates it as "a great prostitute and infamous above all others".[18] However we choose to translate this phrase, it is clear that it holds a negative connotation and hints at debauchery and sexual corruption. Yet the man who reported Francis I's words was known for his strong anti-Boleyn bias and may have exaggerated. Furthermore, his report is inaccurate on many levels, and the Italian original makes it clear he was not even referring to Mary Boleyn.[19]

Many years later, hostile writers asserted that Anne Boleyn also misbehaved while serving Queen Claude. William Rastell, who wrote Sir Thomas More's biography in the 1550s, wrote of how Anne Boleyn was sent to France where "she behaved herself so licentiously, that she was vulgarly called the Hackney of England" and hinted that she became Francis I's mistress and "was termed his Mule."[20] Nicholas Sander, one of the most vociferous critics of the English reformation, embellished the story further, writing: "At fifteen she [Anne Boleyn] sinned first with her father's butler, and then with his chaplain, and forthwith was sent to France, and placed, at the expense of the King, under the care of a certain nobleman not far from Brie."[21] For a brief spell, scholars thought that Sander meant Briare, formerly written Briere, but in the nineteenth century it was established that the town Briare was confused with a small village of Briis-sous-Forges, south of Paris.[22] Sander's story is fabricated, as there is no evidence corroborating his story about Anne's sexual misconduct, but there is a strong local tradition in Briis-sous-Forges, according to which Anne Boleyn lived there. It is especially worth exploring because, as noted by Anne's most eminent biographer, Eric Ives, "Anne Boleyn was to stay with Claude for nearly seven years, a period for which we have no direct evidence."[23] Indeed, in the household accounts of Queen Claude for the years 1515 and 1518, currently preserved in the Bibliothèque Nationale de France, Anne's name is not recorded among the maids and ladies-in-waiting.[24]

Donjon d'Anne Boleyn, Anne Boleyn's Tower, the only remnant of the castle in Briis-sous-Forges that once loomed large over the village, still stands today. A plaque nearby states that Anne lived in the castle with the family of Du Moulin, and a local road is named in her honour. In 1654, historian Julien Brodeau asserted that Anne lived with Philippe du Moulin, seigneur de Brie, but nothing further is known about Anne's links with the family or the castle.[25] It has been recently suggested that it was Mary Boleyn, not Anne, who was sent to Briis-sous-Forges in the aftermath of her alleged affair with Francis I.[26] Perhaps the Boleyn sisters were confused with each other, giving rise to the local tradition in Briis-sous-Forges.

NOTES

[1] Raphael Holinshed, *Holinshed's Chronicles of England, Scotland and Ireland*, Volume 3, p. 611.
[2] Pierre de Bourdeille, seigneur de Brantôme, *The Book of the Ladies*, p. 219.
[3] Cynthia J. Brown, *Like Mother Like Daughter: The Blurring of Royal Imagery in Books for Anne de Bretagne and Claude de France*, p. 121.
[4] *Négociations diplomatiques*, ed. Le Glay, Volume 2, p. 53.
[5] *Travel Journal of Antonio de Beatis*, ed. J.R. Hale, p. 107.
[6] Paul Lacroix, *Louis XII et Anne de Bretagne*, p. 306.
[7] *Letters and Papers,* Volume 2, 1515-1518, n. 647.
[8] *Diarii di Marino Sanuto*, Volume 35, p. 342.
[9] Simone Bertière, *Les Reines de France*, p. 205.
[10] Pierre de Bourdeille, seigneur de Brantôme, *The Book of the Ladies*, pp. 29-30.
[11] Ibid.
[12] Caroline zum Kolk, *The Household of the Queen of France in the Sixteenth Century*, p. 10.
[13] Josephine Wilkinson, *Anne Boleyn: The Young Queen To Be*, p. 35.
[14] Diana Maury Robin, Anne R. Larsen, Carole Levin, *Encyclopedia of Women in the Renaissance*, pp. 173-174.
[15] Ingrid Akerlund, *Sixteenth Century French Women Writers*, p.55.
[16] *Letters and Papers,* Volume 2, n. 4136.
[17] Pierre de Bourdeille, seigneur de Brantôme, *The Book of the Ladies*, p. 220.
The Travel Journal of Antonio de Beatis, ed. Hale, p. 107.
[18] Eric Ives, *The Life and Death of Anne Boleyn*, p. 16. Josephine Wilkinson, *Mary Boleyn: The True Story of Henry VIII's Favourite Mistress*, p. 37.
[19] Read more in *Appendix: Was Mary Boleyn Francis I's mistress?*
[20] Edward, Lord Herbert of Cherbury, *The Life and Raigne of King Henry the Eighth*, p. 258.
[21] Nicholas Sander, *The Rise and Growth of the Anglican Schism*, p. 25
[22] James Gairdner, *Mary and Anne Boleyn*, p. 57.
[23] Eric Ives, *The Life and Death of Anne Boleyn*, p. 29.
[24] *Etat de maison de Claude de France (1514-1515),* BnF, ms.fr. 7853, f. 310, 311-312.
Etat de maison de Claude de France (1518), BnF, ms.fr. 2940, f.48.
[25] Julien Brodeau, *La Vie de Maistre Charles Du Molin*, p. 11.
[26] Alison Weir, *Mary Boleyn: The Great and Infamous Whore*, p. 70.

Chapter 6:
Serving Queen Claude

As Queen Claude's maid of honour, Anne Boleyn was constantly moving between the castles located in the picturesque Loire Valley. "Never during the whole of my embassy was the court in the same place for fifteen consecutive days", wrote the Venetian ambassador.[1] She travelled with Queen Claude and her royal household to various palaces: the St Germain-en-Laye near Paris, where the Queen usually birthed her children; the chateau of Amboise; Plessis-de-Vair in Brittany; and Blois, Claude's favourite residence. To the young and impressionable Anne Boleyn, Amboise was her first taste of luxury and the Italianate style Francis I would later introduce to his other castles in the Loire Valley.

By 1495, King Charles VIII had arranged the transport of works of art from Italy straight to Amboise. These included 130 exquisite tapestries, 172 carpets and 1140 volumes from the famous library of the Aragon kings of Naples, as well as paintings and furniture.[2] Francis I developed a strong desire to accumulate Italian paintings and sculptures and venture on a war campaign there himself one day.

Young and thirsting for glory, Francis soon decided that he would assert himself as a powerful King by conquering Milan. Francis claimed the duchy of Milan in right of his descent from the Visconti dukes—his ancestor was Valentina Visconti—as well as through the fact that both his father and paternal grandfather held the title of the Duke of Milan. Claude was also descended from the same Visconti ancestor, providing a third claim. The duchy had been the possession of the French monarchy for years; Louis XII established Milan as a French capital in Italy in 1500 but lost it to the Sforza family twelve years later. Now Francis decided to reconquer the duchy and return triumphant.

The summer of 1515 saw a slow progress towards the city of Lyons. On the way from Chaumont to Amboise, a thorn injured the King's leg, an accident that Louise of Savoy noted in her journal. "He had much pain", she grievously remarked, "and I too, for true love forced me to suffer the same pain".[3] By 30 June, Francis was with Louise at her little chateau of Romorantin, from whence he departed to Lyons on 4 July 1515 at seven o'clock in the morning. In Lyons, Francis made last preparations for war and declared that "we have decided to leave the government of our realm to our well beloved and dear Lady Mother, the Duchess of Angoulême and Anjou, in whom we have entire and perfect confidence, who will, by her virtue and prudence, know how to acquit this trust".[4]

Louise of Savoy's influence over her son was Anne Boleyn's first lesson in how a powerful woman could rule. "She always accompanies her son and the Queen and plays the governess without restraint", reported one of the observers who was clearly impressed with Louise's personality and appearance.[5] Despite the fact that she was with Claude almost all the time, Louise never took precedence over the Queen, observing correct etiquette on all occasions. At the same time, she was usually present when the Queen received foreign dignitaries. Although herself not a crowned queen, Louise was treated as such by foreign ambassadors and other ruling families who recognised her key role at court and often referred to her, incorrectly, as "Queen Mother".[6]

Whereas Louise of Savoy was given the regency and started carving out a formidable presence at court, Francis's wife was barely noticeable in the early months of her husband's reign. Queen Claude did not take part in the

King's coronation and did not accompany him to Lyons during the summer. The reason she was not present at Francis's coronation, according to Jean Barrillon, secretary of Chancellor Duprat, whose chronicle of the early reign of Francis I is invaluable, was because she was with child at the time. Also, the "heavily pregnant" Claude stayed behind in Amboise on 29 June 1515 when Francis slipped away quietly from the castle and left for Romorantin.[7]

The Queen's first child was born on 19 August 1515 while Francis was waging war in Italy. When he was informed that Claude had successfully given birth to a healthy daughter, he was disappointed because he was hoping for a son. The King's mother, on the other hand, was content because the little princess was named Louise after her. Louise of Savoy recorded in her journal that "Madame Louise, the eldest daughter of my son, was born in Amboise on 19 August 1515 at 10:47 in the morning".[8]

On 13 September 1515, Francis I won the battle against the Old Swiss Confederacy near the town of Marignano, some ten miles southeast of Milan. The victory was so spectacular that Marshal Gian Giacomo Trivulzio, veteran of every war waged for the past forty years, praised Marignano as the "battle of giants" and stated that compared to it, all previous battles in his lifetime had been like "children's games".[9] Back in France, Louise of Savoy was overwhelmed with joy after receiving letters from Francis. The entry in her journal states that she went on foot to the shrine of Notre-Dame des Fontaines to give thanks for the victory and recommend to the care of the saints "him, whom I love better than myself, my boy, glorious and triumphant Caesar, subjugator of the Swiss".[10]

Francis I was back in France in January 1516. Louise of Savoy ordered her daughter, Marguerite, and Queen Claude to gather their retinues and head towards Sisteron, where they were to be reunited with the King. The ecstatic entry in Louise's journal captures her emotions perfectly:

"The thirteenth day of January, my son, returning from the battle with the Swiss, met me near Sisteron, in Provence on the banks of the Durance, at about six o'clock in the evening, and God knows that I, poor mother, was thankful to see my son safe and sound after all he had suffered and endured to serve the common good."[11]

The French King's return offered his wife, mother and sister a chance to make a pilgrimage to the shrines of saints they venerated. The royal women, with their large entourage, left Amboise on 20 October 1515, stopping in various cities for royal entries and celebrations. They spent

Christmas season at Tarascon in Provence, where they visited the tomb of Martha of Bethany, and Arles, where they were shown relics of "Maries de la Mer", Mary Jacobi and Mary Salome. They arrived at Saint-Maximin-la-Sainte-Baume on 31 December, where they made their first recorded visit to the shrine of Mary Magdalene. According to legend, after Christ's death and resurrection Mary Magdalene, Martha, Lazarus, Maximin and other companions went to sea in a rudderless boat, reaching Provence in safety. There, Mary Magdalene converted the people of Marseilles before secluding herself in the cave at La Sainte-Baume, where she survived for thirty years on heavenly sustenance.

Antonio de Beatis, who visited Mary Magdalene's cave in 1517, two years after Anne Boleyn went there with the Queen, described what he saw. His unique eyewitness account gives us a rare glimpse into what the young Anne Boleyn saw when she travelled to the shrine:

"The Sainte-Baume is the highest mountain to be found anywhere in those parts, dominating the whole of Provence and particularly the coastal region. It rises to cliffs of bare rock which soar sheer to a great height, and in the rock face is a great cave where unbeknown to anyone and unseen by human eyes St Mary Magdalen lived as a penitent for thirty years. Here, various rooms have been let into the walls of the grotto and a door added, so as to form a chapel with living quarters and amenities for the friars—Observant Dominicans only five in number—who administer the great shrine. Inside the church one is shown a small cave, now enclosed behind an iron door, where the glorious saint slept for so many years on the bare rock. All who visit the sanctuary as pilgrims are given pieces of the rock to quench the heat of fever, and cords measured against the saint for women in childbirth. The lengths of these cords are taken from a recumbent wooden statue said to have been commissioned by St Maximilian to life-size dimensions. Rain falls everywhere in this cavern-church (although set deep in the rock) except in the cave where the saint used to sleep. There is also a spring of purest water, the state of which never varies, yet the friars and visitors drink from it and use it for washing and all other necessities."[12]

The Queen and royal entourage also visited the Basilica of Saint-Maximin-la-Sainte-Baume which contains the skull of Mary Magdalene. The tomb said to contain Mary Magdalene's remains was found in December 1279 by Charles II of Naples. Antonio de Beatis recorded that:

"In an underground chapel, or rather grotto, beneath the church, the head of the glorious Magdalen is enshrined in a silver casket on the altar, with a silver mask which can be raised showing the head behind a glass cover. Through this one can clearly see that it is quite fleshless apart from the area over the left brow touched with three fingers by Our Lord Jesus Christ when he said 'Touch me not'; and indeed, it is a relic genuine beyond all doubt and most venerable. And from the head (which is very large and has the jaw bone intact and some of the molar teeth)."[13]

Although Mary Magdalene was a favourite saint of the French noblewomen Anne Boleyn served, there was some confusion as to who she really was. The Church tradition had combined three separate women who appear in the Gospels into one highly popular figure. The medieval Mary Magdalene was a combination of a sinful woman, presumably a prostitute, who washed Jesus Christ's feet in the house of Simon the Pharisee; Mary, the sister of Martha and Lazarus at Bethany; and Mary of Magdala, whom Jesus purged of seven devils and who witnessed Christ's death and resurrection and who used expensive ointments to prepare Jesus's body for burial. Medieval and Renaissance periods produced a great number of paintings of women posing as Mary Magdalene, with her unmistakable attribute: an ointment jar.

Louise of Savoy was apparently confused about Mary Magdalene's identity and commissioned Francois du Moulins de Rochefort to write a life of the saint following her visit to Mary Magdalene's shrine. Du Moulins asked Jacques Lefèvre d'Étaples, theologian and humanist, to research the topic and share his thoughts with him. This request prompted d'Étaples to study the saint in great detail and question the well-established image of Mary Magdalene, arguing that she was neither the sinner woman from Luke's gospel nor Mary of Bethany. Anne, like many other women of her period, was fascinated with Mary Magdalene and had an image of the saint in her own Book of Hours.[14]

Francis's triumphant return from war marked a new era for him and his family. The King now needed a male heir who would add lustre to his victory and ensure the succession. In January 1516, Henry VIII decided to brag about his wife's condition in a letter to Francis, writing boldly that Queen Katharine was pregnant and Francis "should put Queen Claude in the like situation".[15] In fact, Claude was already pregnant around that time. Katharine of

Aragon gave birth to Princess Mary on 18 February 1516, crushing Henry's hopes for a male heir yet again. Putting a brave face on, Henry boasted that he and Katharine were still young and "if it was a daughter this time, by the grace of God the sons will follow".[16] Anne Boleyn may have heard that Katharine of Aragon gave birth to a stillborn son in November 1514. Such a tragedy was not only a blow to the royal couple on a personal level, but the lack of a male heir also threatened the stability of the realm. Rumours circulated in France that Henry VIII wanted to repudiate his wife because she was unable to give him a son.

In April 1516, King Francis had a serious accident. According to the Spanish ambassador, he "had a fall from his horse, which made him speechless for an hour". The King survived without any serious damage to his health, and the court returned to its established routine. Later that month, Anne accompanied Claude when "the Queen and my Lady of Angoulême had left Lyons for Amboise".[17] Anne was with the Queen when Claude "began to feel within her body the first movement" of her baby.[18] Although the cessation of menstruation was one of many signs of pregnancy, in an age of no pregnancy tests, women were certain about their condition only after they felt their child's movement, called "quickening", a sign that the child was alive. Princess

Charlotte, the second daughter of Francis and Claude, was born in Amboise on 23 October 1516.

The Queen proved that she was able to provide her husband with healthy children, although she was still under considerable pressure to produce a male heir. Nevertheless, Francis and his mother decided that, considering Claude's enormous popularity, she should be crowned. Claude's coronation took place on 10 May 1517 in the Basilica of St Denis. Anne Boleyn certainly accompanied the Queen since her own coronation in 1533 bore similarities to Claude's entry to Paris. The Queen, wearing a cloak of blue velvet lined with ermine over her shoulders, dazzled the spectators with the richness of her clothes and jewels. On her head, she wore "the most expensive cape" sewn with little leaves of gold onto silver cloth given to her by her mother, Anne of Brittany. During the Mass when *Te Deum* was sung, Claude prostrated herself in front of the high altar, as was customary, and then knelt. She was anointed with holy oil on her forehead, chest and shoulders. During the coronation festivities that stretched over three days, the Queen was celebrated as the "daughter of the most Christian King Louis XII of his name and of Madame Anne of Brittany, twice crowned Queen of France".

On 9 May 1517, Claude paid her respects to her deceased parents, visiting their tomb in the Basilica of St Denis "to pray and say orisons in great devotion and contemplation over the tomb and statue of her father and mother, and not without tears and lamentations".[19]

Several stages with allegorical tableaux vivants, where actors re-enacted highly symbolic scenes, were erected along the Queen's entry route into Paris. Allusions to Claude's mother and her Breton ancestry were present in these scenes, but the Queen was upstaged in the final tableau, which featured a dialogue between St Louis and his mother, Blanche of Castile, emphasising the relationship Francis I shared with his mother rather than with his wife.[20] This tableau reflected the truth. The English ambassador recorded that the King's mother "and my lady of Bourbon [Anne of Beaujeu] bear the rule".[21]

For many centuries, Queen Claude had been hidden behind the stereotype of a royal baby maker. Indeed, she was shy and withdrawn, "a person of few words" with whom "one does not deal with issues of State", as the Venetian ambassador observed after visiting her.[22] But Claude was passionate about one thing: religion.[23] In recent years, scholars drew attention to Claude's personal faith, pointing out that she zealously supported Church reform and held similar religious views as Marguerite of Alençon, her sister-in-law, who was known as a religious reformer. Perhaps if she lived longer, Claude would have been recognised as a religious reformer and shared a similar reputation as Marguerite.[24] Brantôme recorded that Claude "was very good, very charitable, and very gentle to all, never doing any unkindness or harm to anyone either at her court or in the kingdom".[25] She developed the reputation of a pious and docile queen, and her popularity attested to how beloved she was in France.

One of Claude's mottoes, "the firmness of faith doubly increases the hope of eternal life" appealed to Anne, who adopted the armillary sphere, one of the French Queen's emblems, and fittingly placed it under the miniature of resurrection in her own Book of Hours, scribbling "le temps viendra [the time will come], je [me] [armillary sphere] Anne Boleyn".[26] An armillary sphere also appears in her book *The Ecclesiaste* next to her personal emblem of a white falcon.[27] One of Anne's mottoes, "semper eadem", "always the same", may have been inspired by Anne of Brittany's device, "elle ne change pas" which means "she will not change".[28] Claude was familiar with her mother's motto because she used it as a child and continued to use it later in her life. She had it displayed in her Book of Hours, dating to 1517, that still survives.[29]

Shortly after Claude's coronation, tragedy struck: the Queen's oldest daughter, Madame Louise, died on 21 September 1517 at the age of two years. Antonio de Beatis, who saw the little girl during his visit to France, described her as "full of promise".[30] The Queen was four months pregnant when her firstborn daughter died. On 28 February 1518, Claude finally gave birth to her first son, Dauphin Francis, which was the occasion for great rejoicing throughout the entire realm. Claude was so happy that she told the Venetian ambassadors that her son was "even more beautiful" than her husband the King. Francis rejoiced that the newly born dauphin was "the most beautiful and puissant child one could imagine and who would be the easiest to nourish".[31] Louise of Savoy, the proud grandmother, welcomed "the son of my son" with great joy.[32]

Leonardo da Vinci, the great Italian painter and humanist who lived in France at the King's expense, devised pageants for the christening, although he was old and ailing. Francis, fascinated with Italian art, was proud to have Leonardo at his court and gave him the Château du Clos Lucé, located five hundred metres from the royal Château of

Amboise, to which it is connected by an underground passageway, where da Vinci spent his last years. Leonardo was hailed by his contemporaries as "the most outstanding painter of our day", and Anne Boleyn certainly caught a glimpse of him during her time in France.[33] Leonardo's famous *Mona Lisa* was in France at the time when Anne served at court; could she have possibly seen the painting? During her time as queen, Anne adopted "The Most Happy" as her motto. Leonardo's *Mona Lisa* was often called "la Gioconda", meaning "joyous" or "the happy one", because it was a pun on the sitter's last name. Lisa Gherardini, the woman in the painting, was the wife of Florentine cloth merchant Francesco del Giocondo. Could Anne's motto have been inspired by *Mona Lisa*? Anne's motto "The Most Happy" had several meanings. In 16th-century parlance "hap" meant "luck", so by "the most happy", Anne highlighted that she was "the luckiest" of women because she was raised to queenship.

Anne benefitted from Francis I's fascination with everything Italian since the King was eager to order fashionable Italian dresses for the ladies of his court. In 1515, he wrote a letter to Isabella d'Este, Marchesa of Mantua—one of the leading political and cultural figures of the Italian Renaissance—to ask her to send him a fashion doll dressed in the most recent Italian garments so that the ladies of his court could copy her style. Queen Claude also displayed interest in Isabella's style and received three jars of scented hand cream from her.[34]

The birth of the French male heir had an impact on Anne Boleyn's life and career because Francis I and Henry VIII decided to form a marital alliance between their countries. It was agreed that Henry VIII's daughter, Princess Mary, would marry Dauphin Francis. Both kings decided to send embassies to each other's courts. The French embassy to England arrived in the autumn of 1518. On 26 September, Henry VIII, dressed "in very rich attire", formally received the ambassadors.[35] On 3 October 1518, the King swore to the Treaty of London at St Paul's Cathedral during the Mass celebrated by the architect of the alliance, Cardinal Wolsey. Two days later, Princess Mary was engaged to Dauphin Francis. It was a splendid ceremony. Mary, now two and a half years old, was dressed in a robe of cloth of gold with a black velvet cap perched on top of her head and numerous jewels adorning her small person. She was a beautiful and vivacious child, living proof of the King's virility and the Queen's fertility. The ceremony took place in the Queen's chamber at Greenwich, although Katharine of Aragon was not very keen on the French alliance. Nevertheless, the royal couple had unanimously given their consent when the French ambassadors solemnly asked them if they approved of their daughter's match. Henry and Katharine watched as Cardinal Wolsey placed a small ring with a large diamond on Mary's tiny finger. The princess made everyone laugh heartily when she asked Guillame Bonnivet, the proxy groom who slipped the ring down over her second joint, whether he was the dauphin of France because she wished to kiss him. After the ceremony was concluded, feasting and dancing continued into the late hours.

Amongst the conditions of the marriage alliance, the French insisted that Mary should be recognised as Henry VIII's heiress. Unlike in France, women were not debarred from succession in England, but England never really had a successful female ruler, and Henry was haunted by the memory of a dynastic conflict known in history as the Wars of the Roses. His father, Henry VII, won the crown in the Battle of Bosworth, defeating the Yorkist Richard III and establishing the Tudor dynasty. Henry VII merged the warring factions, Lancasters and Yorks, by marrying Princess Elizabeth of York. Their marriage produced several children, including an heir, Prince Arthur, and a "spare", the future Henry VIII.

Prince Arthur married Katharine of Aragon in 1501 but died several months after the wedding. Katharine was way too valuable a catch to be released and sent back to Spain, and she was trapped in England, where Henry VII treated her as a pawn on the political chessboard. After Henry VII's death, Henry VIII married her, claiming that he was fulfilling his father's deathbed wish. By 1518, Henry and Katharine had only one living child together, and the Queen was pregnant again. In the eighth month of her sixth pregnancy, she went into premature labour, and on 9 November 1518 was delivered of a stillborn daughter.[36] This time Henry VIII was not the only one devastated because "never had the kingdom so anxiously desired anything as it did a prince". Had Henry known what the outcome of this pregnancy would be, he would never have allowed for Princess Mary's French match because, as Sebastiano Giustiniani reported, "the sole fear of this kingdom" was "that it may pass into the power of the French through this marriage".[37] This fear was understandable. If the King had no legitimate male heirs, any man who married his daughter could claim England through her. Henry could not come to terms with this thought. In fact, he found it hard to accept that he and his wife were unable to have male children. Although neither

Henry nor Katharine were aware of it, the 1518 pregnancy was Katharine's last and marked the end of her childbearing years.

The Tudor dynasty was endangered not only because Henry VIII had no male heir. Ever since his father ascended to the throne in 1485, the Tudors were haunted by the last Yorkist representatives of the Plantagenet dynasty. Richard III was the last Yorkist king, slain at the Battle of Bosworth, and succeeded by Henry VIII's father. But the Yorkists were still alive and laid claim to the Tudor throne. Henry VII executed Perkin Warbeck, who claimed to have been one of the lost Princes in the Tower, brothers to Elizabeth of York. He also executed Edward, Earl of Warwick, son of George, Duke of Clarence, and Richard III's nephew. But some of the Yorkists were still alive and well.

Richard de la Pole was the most dangerous rival Henry VIII faced in his early reign. He was one of the sons of John de la Pole, second Duke of Suffolk and his wife Elizabeth, sister to Edward IV and Richard III. De la Pole, nicknamed "the White Rose", was hiding in the French town of Metz, located at the confluence of the Moselle and the Seille rivers. Anne Boleyn caught a glimpse of him in June 1516 when de la Pole had an audience with Francis I, Queen

Claude and Louise of Savoy. He "made his lamentation unto them, weeping, saying that he was utterly cast away, and wist [knew] not what to do, and that he had no help of nobody". Francis promised to restore him to the English throne:

"The French King said to him with good comfort, be we not here all three cousins? Think you that we will see you cast away? Nay, nay; but I shall bring you to your right, and help you as much as shall be in our power to do. And bade him make good cheer, and said to him, 'that man that keepeth your realm [Henry VIII] hath dealt so traitorously with me, that I promise you that I shall die for it, but I will put him down and set you in your right'. And so gave him large money, and bade him be of good cheer, and that he should be in areadiness whensoever he should call him."[38]

Henry VIII was desperate to convince Francis I to stop giving shelter to Richard de la Pole and hoped that the new alliance would bring an end to de la Pole's familiarity with the French King. In the autumn of 1518, Henry sent his ambassadors to France. Sebastiano Giustiniani noted that the four English ambassadors departed "with very great pomp, rather regal than ambassadorial, endeavouring in every respect to outvie the French ambassadors".[39] They reached France by 10 December 1518, and two days later they had their first audience with Francis I. On 16 December, the French King ratified the treaty of marriage between the dauphin and Princess Mary.

After the formalities, there was time for pleasure. Anne Boleyn was among the ladies who took part in a great banquet in honour of the English ambassadors that was held on 22 December 1518 in the medieval Bastille fortress dating back to the fourteenth century. The walls were hung with silver and gold brocade, the ceilings were decorated with gilt stars, signs and celestial planets to represent the heavens and the floors were covered with rich carpets. The massive space was lit by torches and chandeliers "throwing such a marvellous blaze of light on the starry ceiling, as to rival the sun".[40] Francis I's sister, Marguerite, Duchess of Alençon, sat on the King's left side during the entertainments. Queen Claude and Louise of Savoy, accompanied by their ladies, observed the spectacle from one of the galleries near the King's dais. Claude was six months pregnant at the time, and this may well explain why she wasn't as prominent as her sister-in-law. Nevertheless, she cut a magnificent figure and overawed the foreign ambassadors with her rich clothes and jewellery. She was "sumptuously dressed with a necklace of innumerable very large pearls, in which sundry very valuable jewels were set".[41] The next day a tournament with banqueting and dancing took place. The Queen and the King's mother again observed everything from the gallery above. Claude yet again dazzled the spectators "dressed in a very rich gown of cloth of gold, lined with very beautiful sables, and a quantity of jewels on her head and neck, and around her waist, so that she quite sparkled".[42]

Anne Boleyn may have been among the thirty "young ladies" who made their sumptuous appearance following the banquet. The Venetian ambassador recorded that "they were all richly dressed in the Italian fashion, in divers colours, with caps on their heads, some being married and some unmarried; and they were dressed by the daughter of Monseigneur Visconti, who was with them; their dresses indeed being rather low in the bodice, and they danced with those lords and barons in the Italian fashion."[43]

In early 1519, Anne's father became the first resident ambassador in France. Previously, both kingdoms exchanged embassies, but they were usually motivated by special events such as the marriage of Mary Tudor to Louis XII in 1514. By 1518, when amicable relations were re-established between the two countries, Henry VIII and Francis I decided that they should have ambassadors residing in their respective countries for longer periods of time.

Boleyn's despatches provide valuable insight into life at Francis I's court and offer a clue to Queen Claude's health. His knowledge of the French Queen's health was gleaned from Anne, who attended Claude on a daily basis. Pregnant for the fourth time, in March 1519 Claude was "very sickly, worse than she has been in any former confinement".[44] This statement points to the fact that Claude's pregnancies were difficult. The young Queen gained more weight with each successive pregnancy, and this put a considerable burden on her already strained body. In addition to uneven hips, Claude also suffered from scoliosis that deepened with each pregnancy.

On 11 March 1519, accompanied by her mother-in-law, the Queen went on a journey to St-Germain-en-Laye, where she was to give birth to her child, but she became ill on the way and was obliged to take temporary lodgings in the village of La Porte de Neuilly. That night Thomas Boleyn learned from Anne that Claude was "in great danger", and the next morning various false reports spread, first about her delivery of a son and then about her death.[45] By late March, Claude was able to finish her travel to St Germain-en-Laye. On 28 March 1519, Louise of Savoy led Thomas Boleyn by the hand to Claude's private chamber, where the pregnant Queen "was accompanied by fourteen or fifteen lords and gentlewomen, in a nightgown, and had nothing upon her head but only a kerchief, looking always her hour when she shall be brought to bed."[46] Three days later, on 31 March, the Queen gave birth to Henri, Duke of Orléans, named after Henry VIII.

While in England etiquette dictated that an expectant mother withdraw from public life about a month before the delivery date, the birth of a royal child in France was a public event and occurred with the nobility and male doctors awaiting news from the birthing chamber right at the door as midwives assisted the Queen. By the eighteenth century, this custom had evolved and royal birth became one of the chief courtly amusements, with nobility—both men and women—inside the birthing chamber observing the process up close. The custom was banned only in 1778 when Queen Marie Antoinette almost died from the lack of fresh air caused by the fact that too many people gathered in her room when she was giving birth to her first child.

On 15 April 1519, Thomas Boleyn reported that a magnificent thanksgiving procession took place at court, "where went in the same King, the Lady his Mother, with all the lords and ladies of the court". The cause of this procession was "to honour the holy cord that our Lord was bound to the pillar with, and many other relics, which were sent to the Queen here from an abbey in Poytow [Poitou] and from divers other places, now when she was delivered of a child".[47] Religious objects were believed to ease pain during labour and help bring forth a healthy child. During this particular procession, the relics were revered, carried on a little cushion and placed on the high altar.

On 5 June 1519, Boleyn sponsored the infant duke in the name of Henry VIII during a magnificent christening. In the course of this grand ceremony, Thomas Boleyn presented a salt-spoon, cup and layer of gold to Queen Claude. Cardinal Wolsey sent a substantial sum of £100 to be distributed as baptismal gifts between the infant's nurse, rocker of his cradle and three gentlewomen of Queen Claude's privy chamber.

In September 1519, the French King had a minor accident when hunting near Blois. He was struck in the face when "riding under a [tree] with a bough", and kept to his chambers.[48] Queen Claude was expecting another child and experienced unpleasant symptoms of early pregnancy, while Louise of Savoy suffered from gout. It may have been during this period, when the royal family was collectively indisposed, that Anne Boleyn formed close ties with two other women at court. The Queen's sister, Madame Renée, was born on 25 October 1510 and was thus about ten years old in 1520. Just like her elder sister, Madame Renée had inherited their mother's uneven hips. Brantôme later wrote that although "she did not have an external appearance of grandeur, her body being weakened, there was so much majesty in her royal face and speech that she showed plainly enough she was daughter of a king and of France".[49] Many years later, when talking about Anne Boleyn with Elizabeth I's ambassador, Renée recalled that "there was an old acquaintance" between herself and Anne, who "was one of my sister Queen Claude's maids of honour".[50] Just how Anne and Renée became friends remains unknown; Renée was much younger than Anne and had her own separate household. It is possible that the two girls bonded over the slight defects both of them had on their hands. Renée had a discoloured nail, and Anne had "some little show of a nail" growing on the side of her finger.[51]

Another woman who made a lasting impression on Anne was the French King's sister, Marguerite. Born on 11 April 1492, Marguerite was well-educated, pious and erudite. She wrote poetry and enjoyed music and dancing but also felt a deep spiritual connection with God. In 1534, Anne wrote to Marguerite that her "greatest wish, next to having a son, is to see you again", hinting at a close connection rather than a casual acquaintance.[52] Although Marguerite had her own household with ladies-in-waiting who served her, she frequented Francis I's court and shared an exceptionally close bond with Queen Claude. A manuscript produced after Queen Claude's death and written in the voice of one of her sons asserted that an alliance linked "the Queen and my aunt".[53] Anne had a lot in common with Marguerite; both shared a love of music and dancing and were keen patrons of religious reformers. Anne's original stance on reform was inspired by Marguerite, who sought the correction of major abuses within the Church. Both women believed in making the Bible available to everyone in the vernacular and thus encouraged its translation.

While serving Queen Claude, Anne also came into contact with the King's mistress Françoise de Foix, Comtesse of Châteaubriant, who served as the chief lady of honour—the highest and most lucrative post—in the Queen's household.[54] Born c. 1495, Françoise was beautiful and learned. Just like Anne, she had dark hair and olive skin and once quoted the biblical Song of Songs, boasting, "black

I am, but beautiful".[55] Francis was attracted by his mistress's dark features and said of her that "Venus was blonde, I've been told: Now I see that she's a brunette".[56] It has sometimes been suggested that Francis was referring to Anne Boleyn, but this is a modern myth. In the nineteenth century, more myths were spread about Anne's sojourn at the French court. In her *Lives of the Queens of England*, historian Agnes Strickland quoted the following passage from what she believed were the memoirs of one Vicomte de Châteaubriant:

"She [Anne Boleyn] possessed a great talent for poetry, and when she sung, like a second Orpheus, she would have made bears and wolves attentive. She likewise danced the English dances, leaping and jumping with infinite grace and agility. Moreover, she invented many new figures and steps, which are yet known by her name, or by those of the gallant partners with whom she danced them. She was well skilled in all games fashionable at courts. Besides singing like a siren, accompanying herself on the lute, she harped better than King David, and handled cleverly both flute and rebec. She dressed with marvellous taste, and devised new modes, which were followed by the fairest ladies of the French court; but none wore them with her gracefulness, in which she rivalled Venus."[57]

Anne was certainly a skilled musician and a fashion icon of the English court, but this description is not a contemporary source. It is still quoted by Anne's biographers although it's been proven to be a hoax.[58] After reading Strickland's biography of Anne, historian John Lingard wrote to a friend in Paris to make extracts for him from the same manuscript source. He learned that the manuscript was actually not a memoir, but a work of fiction written in 1837 and never published. "What a hoax for Miss Strickland," wrote Lingard to his friend John Walker, "it was a historical novel".[59]

Another myth, invented for the purpose of historical fiction but often repeated in nonfiction, is that Anne was well versed in the art of seduction and lovemaking because she had spent seven years in the French court, a place known for lax morals. In Philippa Gregory's *The Other Boleyn Girl*, for instance, Anne catches Jane Seymour on Henry VIII's lap and calls her a "whore", but then Henry comes to Jane's rescue and charges Anne with using "French tricks" on him during their courtship.[60]

In Hilary Mantel's *Bring up the Bodies*, a novel about the fall of Anne Boleyn as seen through the eyes of Thomas Cromwell, Anne's sexuality is a recurring theme. On one occasion, Anne's sister-in-law, Jane Rochford, confides in Cromwell that "before they were married, she used to practise with Henry in the French fashion. You know what I mean".[61] She then goes on to elaborate that Anne "induced Henry to put his seed otherwise than he should have" and that the King "berates her, that she caused him to do so" and thinks it was a "filthy proceeding". This leads Cromwell to the conclusion that Henry VIII regrets lost opportunities for conceiving a male heir with Anne, "seed gone to waste, slid away in some crevice of her body or down her throat".[62] Later in the novel, Henry tells Cromwell that Anne maintained she was "untouched" and he chose to believe her, but now he knew that "she lied to me for seven years that she was a maid pure and chaste".[63]

In both novels, it is Anne Boleyn who is portrayed as the initiator of sexual practices that so outraged Henry VIII. The fictional Anne did so, presumably, to avoid conceiving a child out of wedlock, or to keep Henry at arm's length as long as she could because she knew that when the King finally possessed her, he would quickly lose interest in her. One may say that no importance should be attached to historical fiction because it is, after all, fiction. That is true to some extent. However, the ideas conceived in the realm of fiction often find their way into the collective consciousness, and what started as a fictitious depiction suddenly starts operating as historical "fact". The notion of Anne being sexually experienced or even corrupt because of her stay at the French court is seemingly confirmed in the words of Pierre de Bourdeille, seigneur de Brantôme, who wrote that "rarely or never did any maid or wife leave that court chaste". Historians usually accept that Brantôme was referring to the dissolute court of Francis I, but this is not the case. Brantôme was actually referring to the exploits going on in the household of Jean, Cardinal of Lorraine.[64]

As Queen Claude's maid, Anne was expected to live up to the high moral standards outlined by her royal mistress. As the only Englishwoman in Claude's entourage, Anne also had to contend with the knowledge that she represented her country. Her later refusal to become Henry VIII's mistress may have stemmed from what she learned at Claude's side, as well as from observation of what happened to discarded royal mistresses, whose reputations were often in scandalous tatters after kings got tired of their charms. It is telling that after she became Queen, Anne forbade her male servants to frequent "infamous places" such as "lewd and ungodly disposed brothels".[65] She certainly saw such "ungodly" young gallants in Francis I's court and may even have conceived a strong distaste for men who attended brothels. At any rate, there is no reason to doubt that Anne was truly bent on living a "holy life", as she wrote in a letter to her father.

NOTES

[1] R.J. Knecht, *Francis I*, p. 92.
[2] Colum Hourihane, *The Grove Encyclopedia of Medieval Art and Architecture*, Volume 2, p. 228.
[3] *Journal de Louise de Savoie*, p. 89.
[4] Dorothy Moulton Mayer, *The Great Regent*, p. 86.
[5] *The Travel Journal of Antonio de Beatis*, op.cit.
[6] *Letters and Papers*, Volume 4, n. 5704.
[7] *Journal de Jean Barrillon, Secrétaire du Chancelier Duprat, 1515-1521*, Volume 1, p. 17, 64.
[8] *Journal de Louise de Savoie*, p. 89.
[9] R.J. Knecht, *Francis I*, p. 47.
[10] *Journal de Louise de Savoie*, p. 90.
[11] Ibid.
[12] *The Travel Journal of Antonio de Beatis*, ed. J. R. Hale, p. 156, 157.
[13] Ibid.
[14] BL, King's MS 9, f. 55v: St Mary Magdalene, with a jewelled headdress, sits reading, with an ointment-pot and lid on table. http://www.bl.uk/manuscripts/FullDisplay.aspx?ref=Kings_MS_9
[15] *Calendar of State Papers, Venice,* Volume 2, 1509-1525, n. 680.
[16] Ibid., n. 691.
[17] *Letters and Papers,* Volume 2, n. 1822.
[18] *Journal de Louise de Savoie*, p. 90.
[19] Cynthia J. Brown, *The Queen's Library: Image-Making at the Court of Anne of Brittany, 1477-1514*, p. 55.
[20] Ibid., p. 58.
[21] *Letters and Papers,* Volume 2, n. 1837.
[22] *Calendar of State Papers, Venice,* Volume 2, n. 1271. Kathleen Wilson-Chevalier, *Claude de France and the Spaces of Agency of a Marginalized Queen*, p. 139.

[24] Kathleen Wilson-Chevalier, *Queen Claude de France and Her Entourage: Images of Religious Complaint and Evangelical Reform*, pp. 93-113.
[25] Pierre de Bourdeille, seigneur de Brantôme, *The Book of the Ladies*, p. 219.
[26] A Book of Hours (Bruges c. 1450) owned by Anne Boleyn. Hever Castle, Kent.
[27] James P. Carley, *The Books of King Henry VIII and His Wives*, p. 130.
[28] Joni M. Hand, *Women, Manuscripts and Identity in Northern Europe, 1350-1550*, p. 145.
[29] Ibid., p. 144.
[30] *The Travel Journal of Antonio de Beatis*, p. 131.
[31] *Journal de Jean Barrillon*, Volume 2, p. 78.
[32] *Journal de Louise de Savoie*, p. 90.
[33] *The Travel Journal of Antonio de Beatis*, p. 132.
[34] Yassana C. Croizat, "Living Dolls": *François Ier Dresses His Women*, pp. 94-130.
[35] *Letters and Papers*, Volume 2, n. 1095.
[36] Ibid., n. 1103.
[37] Ibid.
[38] Ibid., n. 2113.
[39] Ibid., n. 4563.
[40] Sebastiano Giustiniani, *Four Years at the Court of Henry VIII*, Volume 2, p. 303.
[41] Ibid., p. 305.
[42] Ibid., p. 307.
[43] Ibid., p. 306.
[44] *Letters and Papers*, Volume 3, n. 111.
[45] Thomas Boleyn to Henry VIII, 14 March 1519, quoted in Elizabeth Benger, *Memoirs of the Life of Anne Boleyn, Queen of Henry VIII*, pp. 116-17.
[46] *Letters and Papers, Foreign and Domestic, Henry VIII*, Volume 3, 1519-1523, n. 189.
[47] Henry Ellis, *Original Letters*, Volume 1, p. 159.
[48] *Letters and Papers*, Volume 3, n. 454.
[49] Pierre de Bourdeille, seigneur de Brantôme, *The Book of the Ladies*, p. 220.
[50] *Calendar of State Papers Foreign, Elizabeth I*, Volume 2, 1559-1560, n. 3.
[51] Eric Ives, *The Life and Death of Anne Boleyn*, p. 40.
[52] *Letters and Papers*, Volume 9, n. 378.

[53] Kathleen Wilson-Chevalier, *Queen Claude de France and Her Entourage: Images of Religious Complaint and Evangelical Reform*, p. 112.
[54] *Officiers des Maisons des roys , reynes , enfans de France et de quelques princes du sang*, p. 313
[55] Kathleen Wellman, *Queens and Mistresses of Renaissance France*, p. 126.
[56] Josephine Wilkinson, *Mary Boleyn*, p. 33.
[57] Agnes Strickland, Elisabeth Strickland, *Lives of the Queens of England*, Volume 2, pp. 571, 572.
[58] Recently repeated as fact in Owen Emmerson, Kate McCaffrey, *Becoming Anne: Connections, Culture, Court*, p. 16.
[59] Edwin Jones, *John Lingard and the Pursuit of Historical Truth,* p. 136.
[60] Philippa Gregory, *The Other Boleyn Girl*, p. 272.
[61] Hilary Mantel, *Bring Up the Bodies*, p. 314.
[62] Ibid., p. 315.
[63] Ibid., p. 346.
[64] Leonie Frieda, *Francis I: The Maker of Modern France*, p. 77.
[65] *William Latymer's Cronickille of Anne Bulleyne*, Volume 30 of Camden Fourth Series, p. 56.

Chapter 7: Anne's last years in France

As resident ambassador, Anne Boleyn's father had an important task to fulfil: to arrange a meeting between Henry VIII and Francis I. The meeting was to take place in the spring or summer of 1520. The English insisted that the meeting should take place in August, but there was a problem. Queen Claude was pregnant again and was expected to be delivered in late July.[1] The French King wrote to Cardinal Wolsey that "he must bring the Queen, who is with child", and the meeting should take place in May.[2] The reason Francis wrote directly to Cardinal Wolsey was that Thomas Boleyn had suddenly been recalled from his ambassadorial post and replaced with Sir Richard Wingfield.

The exact reason Thomas was replaced remains unknown, but some clue is hinted at in the report of the Venetian ambassador in France, written during the previous summer. Giustiniani wrote that Thomas "was the dependant of Madame Margaret [of Austria], to whom he imparted whatever came to his knowledge; on which account great hatred was borne him universally at the French Court".[3] Instructions issued to Sir Wingfield also hint at some disagreeable characteristics of Thomas Boleyn: Wingfield was to "make himself agreeable to all parties". According to one opinion, "Sir Thomas was uncourtly, plodding, business-like, and niggardly; Sir Richard, free, open and liberal".[4] Sir Richard's second wife, Lady Bridget Wiltshire, was to play an important part in Anne Boleyn's later life; they were to become friends, and Bridget would serve as Anne's lady-in-waiting. Her deathbed testimony, whether truthful or invented for the purpose of destroying Anne's reputation, would be used during Anne's trial for adultery in 1536.

Thomas Boleyn took leave of Francis, Claude and Louise of Savoy in February 1520. In a letter to Henry VIII, the King's mother praised Anne's father, informing the English King that "Thomas Boullain has executed his charge very virtuously".[5]

Writing from the French court in March 1520, Sir Wingfield asserted that "great search is made to bring to the meeting the fairest ladies that may be found".[6] Among the ladies who prepared themselves to attend Queen Claude were Françoise de Foix, Diane de Poitiers, Suzanne of Bourbon, Françoise of Vendôme and many others. The French Queen's pregnancy was not enough to persuade Henry VIII to stop asking for a delay. He claimed, somewhat ungallantly, that if Claude delivered her child during the meeting, she would have the honour of Henry and Katharine attending the infant's christening. This was unacceptable, and Francis "marvelled" at Henry's wish to have the meeting postponed, adding that "the time when the Queen may be present has been carefully calculated and cannot be put off for a month".[7] Henry VIII's desire to postpone the meeting was motivated by his great wish to meet with Charles V, Katharine of Aragon's nephew and the newly elected Holy Roman Emperor. In the end, Charles V landed at Dover on 26 May 1520 and left four days later. Henry VIII and his entourage also set sail for France on the same day, arranging another meeting with Charles between Calais and Gravelines, which would follow the meeting with Francis I.

The meeting between Henry VIII and Francis I lasted from 7 until 20 June 1520 in the vale between the village of Guînes, in the English pale of Calais, and the village of Ardres in neighbouring France. The city of tents and pavilions of cloth of gold was created on an empty plain, giving rise to the event's name: "Field of the Cloth of Gold".

This forest of sumptuous structures glistened in the spring sunshine like liquid gold, although the particularly rainy and windy weather forced Francis I to give orders for pulling his tents down after only four days. Rumour had it that when Henry VIII was informed prior to the meeting of how luxurious Francis's tents were to be, he ordered construction of a sumptuous temporary palace with walls of timber painted to look like real brick. Inside the structure there were chambers hung with tapestries and silks inhabited by the royal family and Cardinal Wolsey.

Mary Tudor also accompanied Henry VIII and Katharine of Aragon to the meeting. Despite the fact that she was married to Charles Brandon and had children with him, she chose to emphasise her ties with the French court. Her chambers in Henry VIII's temporary palace were decorated with the letters *M* and *L*, standing for Mary and Louis, joined with golden knots, and hangings embroidered with porcupines, Louis XII's heraldic emblem. The same symbols were proudly displayed on Mary's litter.

For Anne Boleyn the Field of the Cloth of Gold was a rare opportunity to see her family. Her mother, Elizabeth Boleyn, was listed among fifteen baronesses who accompanied Queen Katharine of Aragon, and her father, Thomas, was among numerous knights. Anne's sister, Mary, recorded as mistress "Carie" was among twenty-five "gentlewomen" who attended the Queen.[8] On 20 February 1520, Mary had married Sir William Carey, Henry VIII's gentleman of the Privy Chamber. William, born in 1496, was twenty-four years old.[9] Mary, born between 1498 and 1500, was slightly younger. She was fortunate enough to marry a man her age, and handsome at that. The only existing portrait of William Carey shows a dashing young man with dark hair and eyes, athletic and well-dressed.

Henry VIII and Francis I met for the first time on 7 June 1520. Comparisons between the two monarchs were drawn immediately, and one of the Venetian commentators wrote:

"In stature, beauty, grace and address in jousting there is little difference between them, save that the King of France appears to me rather the taller, and the English King has rather the handsomer face and more feminine, though in truth they are two very fine men and have a splendid retinue."[10]

Francis's retinue was a riot of colour in gold and silver brocades, silks, velvets and satins. Henry's retinue was also superbly dressed and wearing massive gold chains. Visually, there was no great difference between the nations except for the fact that the French turned up in greater numbers. On 9 June, the two Kings and their companies jousted together during the "feat of arms". The next day being Sunday, the King of France went to dine at Guînes with the English Queen, and the King of England came to dine at Ardres with the Queen of France. Francis danced with Anne Browne, who was the mistress of a Frenchman held in England as a hostage after the 1513 war campaign. She was described as "the handsomest in the company" and clearly captured the French King's attention.[11]

The jousts recommenced on 11 June when the Queens and their retinues arrived on the field in richly decorated litters. Katharine of Aragon arrived first, sitting in an open litter covered with crimson satin embroidered with gold. She was dressed in a gown of cloth of gold cut in the Spanish fashion, with tresses of hair cascading down her shoulders. She was accompanied by forty ladies-in-waiting on palfreys and thirty ladies accommodated in six chariots. There are several conflicting reports by Italian observers regarding the English ladies' appearance. Some of them claimed that the Englishwomen were "neither very handsome nor very graceful". The Venetians disparaged their typically English apparel, claiming that they "were not richly clad", while others claimed that the Queen's ladies were "well dressed but ugly".[12] Only one account, that of Governor Triulzi, claimed that the Englishwomen were "superbly arrayed", but not as well as the French ladies, who were unanimously praised for the richness of their apparel and their physical charms.[13] They were "better arrayed and handsomer than the English", wearing gowns of stiff brocade and many costly jewels.[14]

Queen Claude arrived in a litter of cloth of silver wrought with golden knots. She was correspondingly dressed in a cloth of silver gown and wore a necklace of precious stones. In stark contrast to the two Queens, Louise of Savoy—referred to as Madame—travelled in a litter covered with black velvet with "an infinite number of ladies" dressed in crimson velvet with sleeves slashed with cloth of gold.[15] Claude joined Katharine of Aragon on the observation balcony, and after exchanging greetings, they both took their seats upon a wooden stage to watch their husbands jousting at the tilt.

Jousting was a sport that both kings enjoyed and excelled at, although it was a dangerous and potentially deadly pastime. Jousting was the focal point of tournament, which in the Field of the Cloth of Gold also included fighting in the open field and combat on foot at the barriers. In the joust, two fully armoured knights would charge at each other at high speed on either side of a wooden barrier called the tilt, holding a lance in their right hands. They scored high points for breaking their lances against an opponent's body.

On 11 June, it was reported that Henry and Francis jousted for a little more than three hours and "bore themselves valiantly", especially Francis, who "shivered spears like reeds and never missed a stroke".[16] In one encounter, the English King's lance was splintered and his hand sprained. Six days later, on 16 June, Francis was stricken on the temple and eye, either from the spear's impact or his horse's loosened headpiece. He displayed his injuries in front of the Queens and his mother, riding without helmet with a black eye and a black patch.[17] In his *Chronicle*, Edward Hall asserted that Francis I's nose was broken, but this was probably an exaggeration since an injury like that would have been widely commented upon.[18]

The child Queen Claude was expecting was born on 10 August 1520 and christened Madeleine. Her birth was to be the last confinement of Queen Claude's that Anne would attend. In September 1520, a match was proposed between Anne and her distant cousin, James Butler, son and heir of

Piers Butler, Earl of Ormond. Anne's father believed that the earldom of Ormond was his by right since his maternal grandfather, Thomas Butler, seventh Earl of Ormond, died without male issue and he was his closest male relative. Butler, who died in 1515, had only two daughters, one of whom was Thomas Boleyn's mother, Margaret. Piers Butler, a distant cousin of the seventh earl, seized the earldom for himself upon Thomas Butler's death, but Thomas Boleyn was not ready to admit defeat. However, Thomas Boleyn's chances to win the earldom for himself came to nothing, and in the autumn of 1520 a proposal was made to resolve the feud by marrying Piers Butler's son James to Anne. Such a match would ensure that the earldom of Ormond would one day be inherited by a son born to Anne and James, a son with Butler and Boleyn blood running in his veins. Anne would become Countess of Ormond, a considerable advancement in her social position, and live out her days at Kilkenny Castle in Ireland. In September 1520, Henry VIII wrote to Anne's uncle, the Earl of Surrey, "to ascertain whether the Earl of Ormond is minded to marry his son to the daughter of Sir Thomas Boleyn".[19] The negotiations stalled, however, and Anne remained in France.

In early 1521, Anne attended Claude in her private apartments. On 21 February, Sir William Fitzwilliam, the new ambassador, reported that "the French queen has been ill with a rheum in her cheek, and did not come abroad till last night". Fitzwilliam gave her Henry VIII's letter, and Claude said that "she was glad to hear of the King and the Princess" and wished to know more about them.[20] As soon as the Queen regained her health, she intended to go on a pilgrimage with the King's mother. "Today the Queen and my Lady go to Paris to do their pilgrimage", Fitzwilliam wrote on 21 March. Anne was certainly with them—it was to be her last pilgrimage by the French Queen's side.[21]

In November 1521, the match between Anne and Piers Butler's son was revived. Cardinal Wolsey informed Henry VIII that "I will talk with you how to bring about the marriage between his son and Sir Thomas Boleyn's daughter, which will be a good pretext for delaying to send his son over".[22] The last we hear about Anne Boleyn in France is in the letter of the imperial ambassadors residing in England to Charles V:

"The French ambassadors made several complaints about suspiciously unfriendly English acts. All the English students have recently withdrawn from Paris, which, they said, seemed to indicate an English intention to make war on France. Wolsey replied that the students, seeing the confusion in France, were merely consulting their own safety, and could have no idea of Henry's intentions. The ambassadors complained that Boleyn's daughter, who was in the service of the French Queen, had been called home, and said this was not a sign of continued friendship. The cardinal said that he himself was responsible for her recall, because he intended, by her marriage, to pacify certain quarrels and litigation between Boleyn and other English nobles."[23]

Before Anne left France in late 1521, she received a music book from Marguerite of Alençon, the French King's sister. This valuable manuscript, comprised mainly of Franco-Flemish motets, can be firmly linked to Anne because she signed her name there: "Mris [mistress] A Bolleyne / Nowe thus", followed by a musical motto of three minims and a longa. For many years, it's been erroneously assumed that the manuscript was created for Anne and presented during her years as Queen of England, probably by Mark Smeaton, musician of her Privy Chamber. The research conducted by Dr Lisa Urkevich, however, corrected this long-held view. Urkevich argued that the manuscript dates to the early sixteenth century and is of French origin.[24] It remains unknown for whom it was originally created or how many owners possessed it, but one thing remains clear: Anne must have first owned the manuscript when she was young. This is attested by the signature. She signed herself as "mistress" and attached her surname Boleyn to it, together with her father's motto, "nowe thus". This proves that Anne must have been indeed young, still only a "mistress", without fame or distinction, and not a marchioness or queen. Throughout her life, Anne signed her letters as "Anne Boleyn" (before her ennoblement), "Anne Rochford" (from 1529) and "Anne the Queen" (from 1533). It's been credibly suggested that Marguerite gave the manuscript to Anne when she learned of Anne's impending marriage to James Butler—this would explain why Anne signed her name under a song about marriage.[25]

It's also interesting to note that Anne placed her signature beneath the alto part, which may have been the part she sang. People who knew Anne widely commented upon her musical talents, saying that she was skilled "in playing on instruments, singing and such other courtly graces, as few women were of her time".[26] Later in her life she owned a pair of clavichords that she decorated with green ribbon and it was said she "knew perfectly how to sing and dance . . . to play the lute and other instruments".[27] Anne's royal coat of arms and the heraldic device of a falcon decorate the so-called "Queen Elizabeth's virginal" that is currently preserved at the Victoria and Albert Museum in London. It's been suggested by Anne's biographer Eric Ives that this instrument was played by Anne, although recent research proves that the virginal was made c. 1594, long after Anne's death.[28] Still, the link is apparent and may have been Elizabeth's silent tribute to her mother and her musical abilities.[29]

The music book is a rare survivor of Anne Boleyn's early youth and received wide interest due to Dr Urkevich's research as well as Alamire's recording of the chansons in 2015.

_____

NOTES

[1] *Letters and Papers,* Volume 3, n. 549.
[2] Ibid., n. 632.
[3] *Calendar of State Papers, Venice,* Volume 2, n. 1235.
[4] *Letters and Papers,* Volume 3, Preface.
[5] Ibid., n. 664.
[6] Ibid., n. 698.
[7] Ibid., n. 725.
[8] In *The Life and Death of Anne Boleyn*, Eric Ives cleared the controversy over Mary's attendance, p. 371.
[9] His portrait states that he was thirty in 1526.
[10] *Calendar of State Papers, Venice,* Volume 3, 1520-1526, n. 80.
[11] Ibid., n. 50.
[12] Ibid., n. 81.
[13] Ibid., n. 80.
[14] Ibid.
[15] Ibid., n. 84.
[16] Ibid., n. 80.
[17] Ibid., n. 50.

[18] Joycelyne Gledhill Russell, *The Field of Cloth of Gold*, p. 135.
[19] *Letters and Papers,* Volume 3, n. 1004.
[20] Ibid., n. 1161.
[21] Ibid., n. 1202.
[22] Ibid., n. 1762.
[23] *Calendar of State Papers, Spain*, Further Supplement To Volumes 1 and 2, n. 1.
[24] Lisa Urkevich, "Anne Boleyn, a music book, and the northern Renaissance courts: Music Manuscript 1070 of the Royal College of Music, London." PhD dissertation, University of Maryland, 1997.
[25] Lisa Urkevich, *Anne Boleyn's French Motet Book, a Childhood Gift*, pp. 95-119.
[26] William Thomas, *The Pilgrim: A Dialogue*, p. 56.
[27] Susan Walters Schmid, *Anne Boleyn, Lancelot de Carle, and the Uses of Documentary Evidence*, p. 112.
[28] Eric Ives, *The Life and Death of Anne Boleyn*, p. 257.
[29] https://collections.vam.ac.uk/item/O70511/the-queen-elizabeth-virginal-spinet-baffo-giovanni-antonio/

Chapter 8:
"More French than a Frenchwoman born"

The seventeenth-century historian William Camden, who wrote the first biography of Anne's famous daughter, asserted that Anne stayed on in France as maid of honour to Marguerite of Alençon, Francis I's sister, "who was a prime favourer of the Protestant religion then springing up in France".[1] His view may have been influenced by Thomas Wolsey's usher, George Cavendish, who reminisced in his biography of the cardinal that "Mistress Anne Boleyn, being very young, was sent into the realm of France, and there made one of the French queen's women, continuing there until the French queen died".[2] Queen Claude died in 1524, and sources closer to Anne's life place her at the English court in 1522. When Anne returned to England after seven years spent on the Continent, she was said to have been "more French than a Frenchwoman born" and took the English court by storm.

Her match to James Butler never materialised, but Anne quickly caught the attention of other, more prominent, suitors. In her early twenties, Anne was a young lady of refined tastes who more resembled a French noblewoman than an English one. She enjoyed reading books in French, dressed in sophisticated French styles and slipped French mannerisms into conversations. Anne is often credited with introducing French hoods to England, but such a notion is erroneous and can easily be disproved since French fashions were in vogue at Henry VIII's court before Anne's arrival; Katharine of Aragon, for instance, was ordering French hoods for herself and her daughter, Mary, in 1520.[3]

     Anne's perfect command of the French language and the aura of Continental gloss that surrounded her singled her out among English noblewomen, and soon her proud father "made such means that she was admitted to be one of Queen Katharine's maids, among whom, for her excellent gesture and behaviour, she did excel all other".[4] Anne would make an indelible mark on Henry VIII's court, for she was a "wise woman, imbued with as many outward good qualities in playing on instruments, singing and such other courtly graces, as few women were of her time".[5] Anne's talents were noticed, and Katharine of Aragon soon had "this gentlewoman daily attending upon her".[6]

Henry VIII himself dabbled in music and poetry, and he soon started paying closer attention to this "fresh young damsel" who knew how "to sing and to dance". Her "modesty, mixed with a French grace and pleasantness" prompted the King to "fall deeply in love with her".[7] "She could speak French ornately and plain", enthused one contemporary, adding that she was "famed in the court" even before the King noticed her.[8] She was said to have borne "great affection and real passion . . . for the French tongue" and was often seen by others with "some book in French in your [Anne's] hand".[9]

In March 1522, Anne made her official debut at court during the Chateau Vert masque. She was among the eight ladies impersonating qualities that a perfect mistress of chivalric tradition should possess: Beauty, Honour, Perseverance, Kindness, Constancy, Bounty, Mercy and Pity. It is usually assumed that Anne played Perseverance, a role that is historically appropriate for the story of her rise.[10] Contemporary chronicler Edward Hall listed the roles noblewomen played in the Chateau Vert pageant but did not specify who played who. Hall lists: Beauty, Honour, Perseverance, Kindness, Constancy, Bounty, Mercy and Pity.[11] A list of ladies who received costumes they wore as mementoes after the pageant appears to be the source of who played whom:

"These things remain with the French queen, the countess of Devonshire, Mistress Anne Boleyn, Mistress Karre, Mistress Parker, Mistress Browne, Mistress Danet and Mistress [blank]."[12]

Someone has apparently merged these two accounts together, resulting in the assumption that Beauty was played by Mary Tudor (Henry VIII's sister); Honour played by Gertrude Courtenay, Countess of Devonshire; Perseverance played by Anne Boleyn; Kindness played by Mary Carey (Anne's sister); Constancy played by Jane Parker (soon to become Anne's sister-in-law); Bounty played by Mistress Browne; Mercy played by Mistress Danet; and Pity played by an unknown woman. It would not have been impossible for these women to play these exact roles; Mary Tudor, for instance, was praised for her physical attractiveness, so the role of Beauty seems apt. She was also the former queen consort of France and highest in rank; the role of Beauty would have been assigned to her as she was the other women's social superior. Ultimately, however, we cannot be sure who played whom. The ladies wore satin gowns cut in the Italian fashion, close-fitting golden cauls and bejewelled Milan bonnets. Each woman's name was sewn onto her costume for everyone to see.

In the summer of 1523, Christian II, the deposed King of Denmark, arrived in England with his wife, Isabella of Austria. Anne would have remembered Isabella from the court of Margaret of Austria. Christian and Isabella had been exiled from their own dominions and together with their three children sought refuge at the court of Margaret of Austria, Isabella's paternal aunt. Christian requested to see Henry VIII in an attempt to secure his backing in the succession war. They were united by family ties since Isabella of Austria was Katharine of Aragon's niece. They landed at Dover on 15 June 1523 and were "nobly received by the earl of Devonshire, and the bishops of Exeter, and Rochester, and diverse knights and esquires, and so brought to Greenwich: where the King and Queen, standing under their cloths of estate, received [them] in the great hall of Greenwich".[13] Chronicler Edward Hall was not impressed with their entourage "poor and evil apparelled".[14] On 3 July 1523, Cardinal Wolsey wrote that the royal couple was "lodged and feasted at Greenwich, and are now at Bath Place at the King's costs".[15] Henry VIII was eager to help Christian and Isabella return to their country, writing to Charles V, Isabella's brother, that it "would be advisable if the Emperor would join with himself in sending fit persons to Denmark to settle this dispute".[16] The exiled royals were "every day feasted at the court".[17] After twenty-two days in England they returned to Belgium to join Margaret of Austria.

Queen Claude, the woman in whose household Anne spent seven years, died on 26 July 1524. She gave birth to two more children after Anne's departure: a son, Charles, on 22 January 1522, and a daughter, Marguerite, on 23 June 1523. By the time Claude was twenty-three, she was the mother of six children and her health had already begun to deteriorate. Ambassadorial despatches yield evidence of the Queen's constantly ill health, referring to her sicknesses, physicians' visits and the dangers of childbearing. Her physical defects—uneven hips, hunched back and obesity, increasing with each pregnancy—put her life at great risk. In April 1524, Claude's sickness was well-known in ambassadorial circles when the Venetian ambassador wrote that "the Queen of France was very ill".[18] Five months later, the Queen's sister-in-law and Anne's former mentor, Marguerite of Alençon, believed Claude was "gravely ill" as she nursed her through her final sickness.[19]

The court historian Brantôme blamed Claude's philandering husband for infecting her with syphilis, a disease that "shortened her days".[20] Rumours about Claude suffering from "the French pox", as syphilis was popularly called in the sixteenth century, abounded during the months leading up to her death. Many foreign ambassadors wrote that the young Queen "was said to be dying of the [great] pox".[21] In August 1524, Francis I was also rumoured to have been treated for this disease.[22] Shortly after Claude's death it was said that Francis "was much diseased with pox, which malady the late Queen caught from him and died of it".[23]

According to Robert de la Marck, the Queen was sick "for six or seven months" before her death, but in reality her health began to deteriorate in October 1523, which means that she was dying for nine months. Without descriptions of the Queen's symptoms, however, it is impossible to reach a conclusion touching the nature of her last illness.[24] The Queen's death plunged the entire nation into mourning. Robert de la Marck remarked that Francis grieved, and rightly so, because there never had been "a more honest princess on earth, nor one more beloved in all the world, and everyone, young and old, believed that if she had not gone to paradise, then few would go".[25] Apart from the King, his mother and sister were also heartbroken. Anne's reaction to Claude's death was unrecorded, but she must have been aggrieved at the death of a queen to whom she served for so many years.

The Shrovetide joust, which took place on 7 February 1526, is generally accepted as the first indication of Henry VIII's courtly pursuit of Anne Boleyn. During the "solemn joust" described in minute detail by chronicler Edward Hall, Henry VIII led his group of jousters dressed in "cloth of gold and silver richly embroidered". The King displayed a "man's heart" engulfed in flames and a motto *"Declare ie nose"*, which Hall translated as "Declare I dare not".[26] This display of the King's chivalry points to the possibility that he had already tried to make Anne his mistress, but she refused, hence he declared he "dared not" take her virginity away.

Anne was not interested in becoming the King's mistress, but the enamoured King started bombarding her with love letters. The letters, stolen from Anne at some point during the turbulent 1520s, are now currently preserved in the Vatican. They were written in French, the language of Anne's youth. Henry was known for his dislike of penning handwritten letters, but the fact that he frequently wrote to Anne, and in French, strongly suggests he was deeply and madly in love with her. It also suggests that Anne probably felt more at ease speaking and writing in French.

Henry persevered through Anne's refusal and, taking the example of Francis I, offered for Anne to become his maîtresse-en-titre, his official royal mistress:

"But if you please to do the office of a true loyal mistress and friend, and to give up yourself body and heart to me, who will be, and have been, your most loyal servant, (if your rigour does not forbid me) I promise you that not only the name shall be given you, but also that I will take you for my only mistress, casting off all others besides you out of my thoughts and affections, and serve you only."[27]

Although Henry VIII never had an official mistress, always preferring to conduct his affairs in private, Anne Boleyn knew very well what this position entailed. She had been an eyewitness to how Francis I paraded his mistresses at court and how he eventually discarded one after another to pursue new amours. She may well have been wary of becoming a royal mistress after Henry VIII seduced and later abandoned her own sister. Later rumours claimed that Mary Boleyn's son, born during her marriage to William Carey and suggestively named Henry after the King, was a royal bastard. If that was indeed so and her nephew was the

King's child, Anne had yet another reason to shudder at the thought of becoming the King's lover. One contemporary later observed that Anne learned "from the example of her own sister, how soon you [Henry VIII] got tired of your mistresses; and she resolved to surpass her sister in retaining you as her lover".[28] Anne, as intelligent and cunning as she was, was probably aware that sooner or later Henry VIII's sexual desire would wane, and he would tire of her as he did with all the other women in his life, so she decided to adhere to higher moral values and bluntly informed the King that she had "already given my maidenhead into my husband's hands".[29]

For centuries, historians and authors ascribed Anne's reluctance to becoming Henry's mistress to her cold ambition, but it seems more likely that she did what was expected of a lady who was a product of upbringing at the French court. She spent almost seven years serving as Queen Claude's maid of honour, and, although Claude's husband was a notorious womaniser, no one who knew her at the time spoke unfavourably about Anne's early youth. Both English and French courts emphasised that virtue was highly prized. Anne was certainly acquainted with Anne of Beaujeu's *Lessons for My Daughter*, a medieval best-seller and a manual for girls. Anne of Beaujeu advised her daughter and the successive generations of young girls to "devote yourself completely to acquiring virtue". She also advised that a young woman should guard her chastity and "avoid all private meetings" with men because women were often judged and gossiped about even if such meetings were innocent.[30]

Anne Boleyn took these and other tips to heart and refused the King's advances, but it seems highly unlikely that she was hoping that Henry VIII would marry her. This, as recently pointed out by historian George W. Bernard, was not a realistic expectation because the King was already married and a royal divorce seemed unlikely.[31] Nevertheless, Henry VIII was stunned by Anne's refusal and decided to seek the annulment of his marriage to Katharine of Aragon. He and Anne Boleyn were engaged on 1 January 1527, and on 17 May of that year, Henry VIII's "secret matter", as the annulment proceeding came to be known in its early stages, commenced.[32]

The King argued that he had no sons with his wife because Katharine's first husband was Arthur, Henry's elder brother. The Bible prohibited such a relationship, warning that "if a man shall take his brother's wife, it is an unclean thing . . . he shall be childless" (Leviticus 20: 21).

Henry had a daughter with Katharine, but he desperately wanted a son, a male heir who would succeed him and carry his legacy into the next generation and beyond. Anne, much younger than the Queen, promised Henry that she would give him sons. In a Book of Hours she used for devotions, and which she passed to the King on many occasions, Anne inscribed a couplet under the miniature of the Annunciation, the angel Gabriel telling the Virgin Mary that she would bear a son: "By daily proof you shall me find to be to you both loving and kind".[33]

Henry VIII wanted to keep his relationship with Anne Boleyn secret for obvious reasons. Had anyone learned that he sought divorce only to marry the Queen's maid of honour, the divorce case would have been lost before it had even begun. During the early stages, this strategy evidently worked. Henry allowed himself to appear in public with Anne on 5 May 1527 when the two danced together at the court ball at Greenwich. It was not an unusual thing for the King to dance with one of the Queen's ladies, and it is unlikely anyone suspected that Henry and Anne were already engaged. But Anne's presence did not pass unnoticed. The French ambassador, to whom Anne was a familiar figure, reported that:

"We were in the Queen's apartments, where there was dancing, and M. de Turenne, on the King's command, danced with Madame the Princess [Henry VIII's daughter, Mary] and the King with Mistress Boulan, who was brought up in France with the late queen."[34]

On 13 July 1527, the Spanish ambassador Don Inigo Lopez de Mendoza reported that Henry VIII's intended divorce "is as notorious as if it had been proclaimed by the public crier", but it wasn't until 16 August that he learned that "it is generally believed that if the King can obtain a divorce, he will end by marrying a daughter of Master Boleyn, who was once ambassador at the imperial court, and who is now called Milord Rochford".[35] Anne had thus stepped out of obscurity and into the spotlight, although it was not yet the kind of notoriety she would gain in the years to come.

When Cardinal Wolsey, Henry VIII's chief advisor and chancellor, learned about his sovereign's divorce plans, he started thinking about a possible bride for his master. Over a year later, Wolsey had even alleged, in a conversation with the French ambassador, that he was responsible for the instigation of Henry VIII's divorce in order to break the imperial alliance and bring about a union between England and France.[36] This was clearly not the case as evidenced during the Blackfriars Trial of 1529 when Wolsey requested the King "to declare before all this audience, whether I have been the chief and first mover of this matter unto your majesty, or no: for I am greatly suspected herein".[37] Henry admitted that Wolsey was at first against such proceedings, and it was the question posed by the Bishop of Tarbes, one of the French ambassadors, in the spring of 1527 that prompted him to question the validity of his marriage to Katharine of Aragon and therefore their daughter's legitimacy. Henry adamantly claimed that over the course of betrothal negotiations for Mary and Francis I's son, the bishop enquired whether Mary was legitimate because Henry "begat her on his brother's wife, which is directly against God's law and his precept".[38]

Wolsey, anti-imperial and strongly pro-French in his political sympathies, decided that Henry VIII should marry a French bride after his divorce from Katharine of Aragon. Gossip among the foreign ambassadors had it "that the Chancellor, by advocating this divorce, is anxious to bring about the marriage of Henry with Madame Renée".[39] "I think his idea was, if this divorce took place", the French ambassador later wrote, "that he would fall back upon

Madame Renée".[40] Indeed, such rumours circulated around the time of Wolsey's embassy to France. Shortly before he was sent there in the summer of 1527, Wolsey met with the Hungarian ambassador Jerome Lasco, who had recently returned from the French court, and talked to him about the current political situation. Lasco was instructed by his master, John Zápolya, to enter the negotiations "with the French King upon alliance and marriage with Dame Renée, having ample instructions to conclude the same". Lasco didn't open the negotiations because he was disappointed when he set eyes on Renée, whom he deemed "not meet to bring forth fruit, as it appeared by the lineation of her body".[41]

In the end, Wolsey never talked with Henry VIII about the intended marriage to Renée because he, like Jerome Lasco, realised that Henry needed, above all, a noblewoman with an unquestioned ability to bear him sons, and Renée appeared unable to bear children. But wild rumours swirled at both courts. According to Wolsey's gentleman usher George Cavendish, "a certain book" was printed and shipped off to England. This "book", a derogatory pamphlet, proclaimed that Wolsey went to France in order to arrange two marriages: one between Princess Mary and Francis I's second son, the Duke of

Orléans, and "one between the King our sovereign lord and Madame Renée".[42] It was only after Wolsey returned to England in September 1527 that he realised that Henry VIII already had a bride in mind. That future bride was Anne Boleyn.

Wolsey now quaked in his shoes because Anne was a friend and supporter of the French policy, and she was no friend of his; he now became expendable. After his downfall, largely engineered by Anne and her faction, the imperial ambassador Eustace Chapuys observed that the King of France had lost nothing by Wolsey's downfall because he now had Anne as the greatest supporter of the French policy at Henry VIII's court. A natural Francophile, Anne was inclined to seek an alliance with Francis I rather than the one with Katharine of Aragon's nephew Charles V. Anne had enjoyed greater favour than Wolsey ever did, and, Chapuys remarked, King Francis was not obliged to pay her an annual pension of twenty-five thousand crowns as he did to the cardinal, "but pays her only in flattery and in promises of forwarding the divorce at Rome".[43]

In the meantime, Anne's old acquaintance Renée married Ercole d'Este, Duke of Ferrara, on 28 June 1528. The Venetian ambassador, overawed by the spectacle, wrote that "Madame Renée has been married in regal attire in the fashion of the Queens of France . . . She wore on her head the crown of a Queen, and an infinity of jewels, and a pectoral adorned with so many emeralds and diamonds that they were worth a kingdom; and she was led to and from the church by the hand by the Most Christian King".[44] Renée's court in Ferrara would become a safe haven for Protestants escaping France. Anne must have followed Renée's story with interest. The duchess gave birth to five children over the years, proving her critics wrong. Brantôme, aware that this was a great accomplishment considering Renée's bodily restrictions, paid her the ultimate compliment when he wrote that "like her sister Claude, she was fortunate in her issue, for she bore to her husband the finest that was, I believe, in Italy, although she herself was much weakened in body".[45]

While Renée had successfully entered into her childbearing years, Anne Boleyn complained that she was losing her time and youth "for no purpose at all".[46] The imperial ambassador, with a streak of malicious glee, reported that Anne, who was nearing her thirtieth birthday, bitterly complained that she had been "waiting long and might in the meanwhile have contracted some advantageous marriage, out of which I might have had issue, which is the greatest consolation in this world".[47] She had reason to complain because by 1531 Henry VIII's divorce case had reached a stalemate, and both he and Anne started losing hope.

Furthermore, Anne's reputation lay in scandalous tatters because she had gained notoriety in England as well as throughout the courts of Europe and was branded as the King's mistress and a whore. Dr Pedro de Garay, Charles V's correspondent, wrote:

"What the King ought to have done was to cast away from him, and from the service of his Queen, the lady [Anne Boleyn] who is the cause of all this evil. She might have been disposed of in marriage, or shut up in a convent, or sent to Madame [Margaret of Austria] with a post of honour in her household. This being done, and the King fasting for several days upon bread and water, with severe penance besides for the scandal given, he should then have commended himself to God and placed the affair in the hands of His Holiness, the only authority in such matters. I would consent to lose my head on the block, if after a month of such a life the King did not become a better husband than ever he was before, and retrieve his soul, ensure his estate, and restore the Queen in all her rights so unjustly taken away from her. Should he do that he would no longer suffer from scruples, and everyone would consider him a good Christian."[48]

There is no information as to whether Margaret of Austria was willing to accept Anne as her maid of honour again, but Anne was certainly not interested at this point. She would either marry the King or no one at all since her reputation was all but ruined. Anne certainly fondly remembered her Habsburg mentor, even if Margaret allied with her former sister-in-law, Katharine of Aragon. Margaret learned of the King's intention to divorce Katharine of Aragon in August 1527 and sided with the Queen immediately, sending her words of comfort and lawyers from the Netherlands.[49]

When Margaret of Austria died on 3 December 1530, three years into Henry VIII's divorce case, the King was relieved. According to Eustace Chapuys, the imperial ambassador, Henry had "shown pleasure" at Margaret's death and proclaimed that "it was no great loss for the world". Chapuys speculated that one of the reasons Henry was so glad of the archduchess's death was because "she took great interest in the Queen's matter" and because it was Anne who made him speak in such an "inconsiderate a manner".[50] If this is any indication of Anne's reaction to her former mentor's death, we may assume that she also felt relieved that one of Katharine of Aragon's staunchest supporters had died, although Chapuys cannot be fully trusted as he often blamed Anne for the slightest changes in Henry VIII's mood or in politics in general.

Some indication of Anne's feelings after Margaret's death can be found in the new motto she adopted in December of 1530. Anne had her servants' liveries embroidered with "Ainsi sera groigne qui groigne", "Let them grumble; that is how it is going to be".[51] The motto emphasised Anne's feelings about her personal relationship with Henry VIII and her opinion about the policies recently adopted by the King. The motto was also a play on Margaret of Austria's "Groigne qui groigne, vive Bourgogne!" which means "Grudge who grudges, long live Burgundy!" By the end of December 1530, however, Anne had removed the motto from her servants' liveries. Chapuys took it as an indication that Anne was not aware of its imperialist origin, but the more likely explanation is that she deemed the motto too bold and perhaps disrespectful, considering the recent death of Margaret of Austria.[52] Even if Anne's motto lasted for only several weeks, it inspired a carol, perhaps written by poet Thomas Wyatt, who was enamoured with Anne. Since one of the stanzas pre-echoes Anne's motto

"The Most Happy" ("But makes me happiest that ever was"), it is possible that she herself was the author of the carol. The piece opened with "Grudge on who list, this is my lot", an "unmistakable translation" of Anne's "Let them grumble" motto.[53]

As more time passed, Anne became angry with the pope for delaying his verdict on the King's marriage. While Henry VIII was eager to wait for the pope's final verdict on his marriage to Katharine of Aragon, Anne started devising other solutions. She leaned towards evangelical religious views and managed to show Henry her own copy of William Tyndale's *The Obedience of a Christian Man*. In this book, labelled as heretical and banned in England, Tyndale argued that popes had no authority over kings, a controversial view that was eminently suitable in Henry VIII's situation. Apart from that, Tyndale also argued that the Bible should be available to every man in his own tongue, an argument that Anne Boleyn had enthusiastically adopted when serving at the French court, influenced by Marguerite of Alençon. But Henry's mind was not there, or at least not yet. Deeply attached to Catholic principles, Henry VIII believed that the pope would eventually rule in his favour. For that, Henry thought, the pope needed a little extra push from none other than his Most Christian Majesty Francis I.

Francis was now the only ally who could help Henry solve his matrimonial problems, and the King decided to renew the Anglo-French alliance. In December of 1530, Henry sent Anne's brother and Anthony Browne "to be present at the Queen's coronation and has provided each of them with £1,000 sterling for their expenses".[54] Francis had recently married Charles V's elder sister, Eleanor of Austria, who was to be crowned in March 1531. Francis didn't want to marry Eleanor, but the marriage was the only way Charles V would agree to release the French King's sons from captivity after they were taken hostage in Francis's place in 1526. Anne had known Eleanor at the court of Margaret of Austria and perhaps hoped that they could establish an amicable relationship—a misplaced hope as Eleanor would never accept Anne as her equal.

In 1532, Henry VIII decided to repeat the Field of the Cloth of Gold, only this time he would not take his wife with him. Instead, Henry ruled, Anne Boleyn would go and be presented to the French nobility as his future wife. For her part, Anne hoped that Calais—where the two monarchs were to meet—would be the stage of her great triumph.

NOTES

[1] William Camden, *The History of the Princess Elizabeth Late Queen of England*, p. 3.
[2] George Cavendish, *The Life of Cardinal Wolsey*, p. 120.
[3] Maria Hayward, *Dress at the Court of King Henry VIII* p. 172.
[4] George Cavendish, *The Life of Cardinal Wolsey*, p. 120.
[5] William Thomas, *The Pilgrim: A Dialogue*, p. 56.
[6] George Cavendish, *The Life of Cardinal Wolsey*, p. 131.
[7] William Camden, op. cit.
[8] William Forest, *The History of Grisild the Second*, ed. William Dunn Macray, p. 53.
[9] Eric Ives, *The Life and Death of Anne Boleyn*, p. 269.
[10] In *The Life and Death of Anne Boleyn* (p. 37), Ives calls them "roles of historical appropriateness."
[11] Edward Hall, *Hall's Chronicle*, p. 631.
[12] *Letters and Papers, Henry VIII,* Volume 3, 1519-1523.
[13] Edward Hall, *Hall's Chronicle*, p. 658.
[14] Ibid.
[15] *Letters and Papers,* Volume 3, n. 3153.
[16] Ibid., n. 3155.
[17] Edward Hall, *Hall's Chronicle*, p. 658.
[18] *Calendar of State Papers, Venice,* Volume 3, n. 819.
[19] Guillaume Briçonnet, Marguerite d'Angoulême, *Correspondance (1521-1524),* Volume 2, p. 64.
[20] Auguste Cullerier, *De quelle maladie est mort François Ier*, p. 11.
[21] *Calendar of State Papers, Spain*: Further Supplement To Volumes 1 and 2, entries for 30 March and 15 April 1524.
[22] *Letters and Papers, Foreign and Domestic, Henry VIII,* Volume 4, 1524-1530, n. 606.
[23] *Calendar of State Papers, Venice,* Volume 3, n. 1066.
[24] The seventeenth-century historian Scévole de Sainte-Marthe claimed that Claude suffered from a skin condition referred to as "une espèce de darte", which her doctors didn't know how to cure. Georges Touchard-Lafosse, *Histoire de Blois*, p. 154.
[25] Robert de La Marck, seigneur de Fleuranges, *Mémoires du maréchal de Florange, dit le Jeune Adventureaux*, Volume 2, p. 148
[26] Edward Hall, *Hall's Chronicle: Containing the History of England,* pp. 707-708.
[27] Ibid.
[28] Reginald Pole, *Defence of the Unity of the Church*, p. 185.

[29] BL, Sloane MS 2495, f. 3, quoted in Eric Ives, *The Life and Death of Anne Boleyn*, p. 84.
[30] Sharon L. Jansen, *Anne of France: Lessons for My Daughter*, p. 40.
[31] George W. Bernard, *Did Anne Boleyn Crave the Crown?*, BBC History Magazine, June 2015.
[32] I follow Dr David Starkey's dating of Henry VIII's engagement to Anne Boleyn (Starkey, *Six Wives: The Queens of Henry VIII*, p. 282).
[33] BL, King's MS. 9, f. 66v.
[34] David Starkey, *Six Wives: The Queens of Henry VIII*, p. 286.
[35] *Calendar of State Papers, Spain,* Volume 3 Part 2, n. 113, 152.
[36] *Letters and Papers, Foreign and Domestic, Henry VIII,* Volume 4, 1524-1530, n. 4865.
[37] Edward Hall, *Hall's Chronicle*, pp. 754-756. Charles Dodd, *Dodd's Church History of England*, p. 186, 190.
[38] Ibid., p. 187.
[39] Jean Marie Vincent, *The Life of Henry the Eighth: And History of the Schism of England*, p. 159.
[40] *Letters and Papers, Foreign and Domestic, Henry VIII,* Volume 4, 1524-1530, n. 4649.
[41] *State Papers Published Under the Authority of His Majesty's Commission King Henry the Eighth: Parts 1 and 2,* Volume 1, p. 203.
[42] George Cavendish, *The Life of Cardinal Wolsey*, p. 118.
[43] *Calendar of State Papers, Spain,* Volume 4 Part 2, 1531-1533, n. 995.
[44] Marino Sanuto, *I Diarii di Marino Sanuto*, Volume 48, p. 233.
[45] Pierre de Bourdeille, seigneur de Brantôme, *The Book of the Ladies*, p. 220.
[46] Eric Ives, *The Life and Death of Anne Boleyn*, p. 128.
[47] Ibid.
[48] *Calendar of State Papers, Spain,* Volume 4 Part 1, n. 463.
[49] *Letters and Papers,* Volume 4, n. 3340.
[50] *Calendar of State Papers, Spain,* Volume 4 Part 2, n. 584.
[51] Ibid., Volume 4 Part 1, n. 547.
[52] Paul Friedmann, *Anne Boleyn*, Volume 1, p. 128.
[53] Richard Leighton Greene, "A Carol of Anne Boleyn by Wyatt", *The Review of English Studies*, New Series, Vol. 25, No. 100 (Nov., 1974), pp. 437-439.
[54] *Calendar of State Papers, Spain,* Volume 4 Part 1, n. 547.

Chapter 9:
Back in Calais

In 1532, Anne Boleyn was at the apogee of her power and influence. On 23 June, the mutual peace treaty between England and France was signed, and on 1 September, Anne was made Marchioness of Pembroke, a peeress in her own right with a substantial annual income of £1,000 per year.[1] She feted the French ambassador, Gilles de la Pommeraye, in her newly acquired and splendidly decorated house at Hanworth and invited him on a hunting expedition, where she presented him with a coat, a hat and a greyhound. Shooting at deer with crossbows—a sport that Anne particularly enjoyed—they talked about current politics and the upcoming interview with Francis I. Anne made sure the ambassador knew that she played the key role in convincing Henry VIII to cultivate his alliance with France. De la Pommeraye quickly sensed Anne's true intent:

> "The greatest pleasure that the King of France can do to this King [Henry VIII] and Madame Anne, is to ask the King to bring Madame Anne with him to Calais, so that they may not be there without ladies, but then the King must

bring the Queen of Navarre [formerly Marguerite of Alençon] with him to Boulogne."[2]

The imperial ambassador Chapuys heard similar reports. The King desired Francis I's sister, Marguerite, now Queen of Navarre, to be present during the meeting to greet Anne and show to all the world that Anne was accepted as the future Queen of England. This was not to be, however. Henry was angry because Marguerite was "indisposed and unable to attend"; she would not greet the King of England's mistress, as Anne was perceived by the French nobility.[3]

Henry could hardly blame Francis for not bringing Marguerite with him because his own sister also refused to accompany Anne Boleyn. In April 1532, Mary Tudor Brandon publicly referred to her former maid of honour using "opprobrious language", causing a stir at court.[4] There was no love lost between the two women. Mary was not only loath to acknowledge Anne as the King's future wife, but also refused to bow to her former servant. She was raised on old values; servants had to know their place, and Anne had blatantly turned the social order upside down. Anne was the one who was paraded at court as if she were already Queen, occupying the consort's throne while Katharine of Aragon was exiled, and taking precedence over all other noblewomen, including Mary herself. As a crowned

Queen of France, Mary was adamant in not tolerating this and chose a domestic life with her children rather than attending court, where she had once shone along Katharine of Aragon and Princess Mary, taking part in banquets, masques and tournaments. Mary blamed Anne for sowing discord in the royal family, and when the King's sweetheart attacked Mary's husband, Charles Brandon, all hopes of reconciliation disappeared.

Charles Brandon was among a small group of intimates who dared to speak openly with Henry VIII. He had once told the King that there was an intimate relationship between Anne Boleyn and an unidentified member of the court in the past.[5] Whatever this relationship's nature, it appears that Henry knew about it from Anne, but Brandon was nevertheless briefly banished, although he quickly returned to the King's good graces. Anne wasn't as forgiving as Henry and accused Brandon of having "criminal intercourse with his own daughter".[6] Whereas Brandon was able to put his grievances aside, or so he pretended, his wife defied Anne Boleyn until her death in June 1533.

Despite the fact that the sisters of Henry VIII and Francis I refused to entertain her in Calais, Anne made the necessary preparations for the journey. The King ordered "rich and most expensive dresses and ornaments" for her and commanded Katharine of Aragon to yield her royal jewels. At first, the Queen refused to countenance the outrageous prospect of giving up her jewellery "for such a wicked purpose as that of ornamenting a person who is the scandal of Christendom", but when she received a formal order signed by Henry VIII, she agreed out of wifely obedience. Soon Anne was parading in the Queen's rings, necklaces and bracelets, setting tongues wagging—even the French King had never presented his mistresses with valuables belonging to his wives.[7]

Amidst all the intense preparations, Anne chose to ignore the fact that it was agreed that there would be no ladies in Calais to greet her on French soil. The imperial ambassador Chapuys thought that after this decision was made, the meeting between Henry VIII and Francis I would be an all-male assembly. He was thus surprised when he learned that Anne was busy sending invitations to her favourite ladies to attend her in Calais.[8] Anne confessed to one of her closest friends that she wished that all of her dreams would come true there. Some took it as a sign that Anne was talking about marriage to Henry, and indeed Katharine of Aragon feared that her husband might make her his wife while in France. As it soon became apparent, Anne was not talking about marriage because "even if the King wished to marry her now, she would never consent to it, for she wants the ceremony to take place here, in England, at the usual place appointed for the marriage and coronation of Queens".[9] She was talking about the consummation of her relationship with the King.

Anne's enemies believed that most of her elaborate preparations had proved in vain, for no suitable royal lady in France was willing to receive her. Henry VIII made it clear that Francis's second wife, Eleanor, was not welcome because she was Charles V's sister. The King quipped that seeing Eleanor dressed in Spanish fashions would be like seeing the "Devil in a woman's dress".[10] Even if she wanted to be in Calais to obey her husband, Eleanor was in no way fit to travel because at the end of September 1532 she miscarried a child, and Francis hastened to her side, spending several days in her company before leaving for Paris and then for Boulogne and Calais.[11]

In the end, there were no women on the French side. Francis suggested that one of the leading noblewomen of his court, Françoise of Alençon, Duchess of Vendôme, should come, but this idea was quickly discarded when it became apparent that the insolent duchess planned to bring with her companions of bad reputation to insult Anne Boleyn. Anne seemed to be undeterred and took thirty noblewomen of her own, among them seven of her family relations.

By ten o'clock on the crisp morning of 11 October 1532, Anne Boleyn and Henry VIII arrived on board the *Swallow* from Dover. Acknowledging Anne's presence, the French King sent her pears and grapes through Anne de Montmorency, the Grand Master of France. On 21 October, Henry rode off to spend four days with Francis in Boulogne, leaving Anne behind in Calais, lodged comfortably in the Exchequer. On Friday, 25 October, the two monarchs came to Calais, where it was the English King's turn to entertain.

The French King, paying compliment to her yet again, sent Anne a jewel worth a staggering amount of £3,500. Two days later, she thanked him in person when, making a spectacular entry with seven other ladies, she performed her bewitching dance. All masked and "gorgeously apparelled" in costumes of "strange fashion", each of the ladies singled out French gentlemen to dance with. Anne, naturally, claimed King Francis. After a couple of dances, Henry VIII approached the dancers, taking the visors off all the masked ladies. Dancing continued while

Francis led Anne to a window embrasure, where they talked for about an hour until the banquet was over. On Tuesday, Francis left for Paris. Anne and Henry lingered in Calais, prevented from crossing the Channel by unfavourable, stormy weather. They left on 12 November 1532.[12]

Both Henry VIII and Anne Boleyn believed that Calais was an unqualified success, but it later became apparent that Francis I entertained a different opinion, telling the pope over a year later that he tried to dissuade Henry from marrying Anne or at least tried to convince him to wait for some time until a set of more favourable circumstances would emerge.[13] But Henry could not wait much longer. According to chronicler Edward Hall, the couple married in secret on 14 November upon landing in Dover. They consummated their relationship and in December Anne became pregnant. It is highly likely that Anne became formally betrothed to Henry in November because while in Calais she lambasted the King's representative in Rome, Sir Gregorio Casali, "for not managing her affair better; for she had hoped to be married in the middle of September."[14] On 25 January 1533 rumours swirled at court that Henry VIII married the already pregnant Anne Boleyn, hoping that the pope would eventually sanction his new marriage. This second ceremony was also secretive.

Two months later, in March 1533, Henry appointed Anne's brother as ambassador to the French court. George Boleyn was to announce to Francis I that his master, according to the French King's advice given in Calais, as well as because he wished to have male issue, had married Anne and intended to crown her. George was to emphasise that Henry expected that Francis's "deeds will correspond with his promises" and that the French King would intercede with the pope on Henry's behalf.[15]

The marriage in itself did not mean that Henry broke with the Catholic Church; he now wanted his ambassadors in Rome to convince Pope Clement VII that the divorce should be tried in England, not in Rome. When this plan turned to ashes after the pope allied himself with Charles V, Katharine of Aragon's nephew, Henry began efforts to strengthen his own authority and annul his first marriage. On 23 May 1533, the new Archbishop of Canterbury, Thomas Cranmer, declared Henry's first marriage null and void, arguing that his marriage to Anne Boleyn was valid because the King had been free to remarry all along.[16] Katharine of Aragon was given a new title:

Princess Dowager of Wales, but it changed nothing in her perception of her royal dignity.

On 1 June 1533, Anne Boleyn was crowned, and although she looked splendid in her overdress and mantle of cloth of tissue furred with ermines, people refused to exclaim the customary "God save the Queen" as she passed. The French ambassador Jean de Dinteville, who accompanied her through the crowded streets of London, was abused with insults; people called him a "French dog" and a "whoreson knave".[17] Anne's Frenchness now became a disadvantage in the eyes of the English subjects, who feared that their King would be excommunicated and their country invaded by Charles V's forces.

On 7 September 1533, Anne Boleyn gave birth to a daughter, Elizabeth, dashing Henry VIII's hopes for a son. Later that autumn, Francis I met with the pope in Marseilles and, according to the stipulations of the Franco-Papal alliance, married his son Henri to Clement's niece, the fifteen-year-old Catherine de Medici. Henry felt betrayed because Francis had promised him in Calais that he would not marry his son to the pope's niece unless and until Clement VII granted Henry his longed-for divorce. Francis argued that "he had promised the Pope for a long time to make this marriage", but Henry was outraged and during a parting audience with the French ambassador Dinteville accused Francis of double-dealing.[18]

Anne Boleyn, on the other hand, believed that the Anglo-French relations could be mended and spoke in favour of the French.[19] When the new French ambassador arrived in December 1533, it was Anne who made sure that Jean du Bellay felt welcome. She made him a very gracious reception and kissed him on the cheek when he presented her a letter from Francis.[20] Anne had high hopes for the French alliance and saw herself as a nourisher of peace between the two nations. The crowning achievement of her ambitions was to see her infant daughter, Elizabeth, matched to Francis I's youngest son, Charles.

Although Elizabeth was not the longed-for male heir, Anne was nevertheless a proud mother who took a keen interest in her daughter's upbringing. When she was three months old, Elizabeth was placed in her own establishment, where an array of governesses, wet nurses and rockers tended to her every need. As Queen, Anne was not expected to raise her daughter, but she was a constant presence in Elizabeth's life. Whenever the child came to visit her parents in the royal palaces, Anne sat on a throne under a canopy of estate while Elizabeth was placed on a richly embroidered cushion next to her so that everyone might look upon this new princess of England.[21]

In the spring of 1534, Anne made sure that the three French ambassadors paid a visit to her daughter and reported to Francis I that she was a healthy and lively child. Castillion, Morette and La Pommeraye witnessed Elizabeth presented to them "in very rich apparel, in state and triumph as a Princess, and afterwards they saw her quite naked".[22] This show had its own purpose because by March 1534, Henry VIII had completed his break from Rome and passed the new Act of Succession, designating his daughter by Anne Boleyn and any subsequent sons they might have as heirs to the throne. Now Queen Anne had to succeed where her predecessor had failed and deliver a male heir.

NOTES

[1] This was an enormous sum of money. Anne earned more than speakers of the House of Commons, who usually received £100 per year.
[2] *Letters and Papers, Foreign and Domestic, Henry VIII,* Volume 5, 1531-1532, n. 1187.
[3] *Calendar of State Papers, Spain,* Volume 4 Part 2, 1531-1533, n. 1003.
[4] *Calendar of State Papers, Venice,* Volume 4, 1527-1533, n. 761.
[5] *Calendar of State Papers, Spain,* Volume 4 Part 1, Henry VIII, 1529-1530, n. 302. Historians identify this gentleman as Thomas Wyatt.
[6] Ibid., Volume 4 Part 2, 1531-1533, n. 765.
[7] *Calendar of State Papers, Spain,* Volume 4 Part 2, 1531-1533, n. 1003, 1047.
[8] Ibid., n. 986.

[9] Ibid., n. 824.
[10] *Letters and Papers, Foreign and Domestic,* Henry VIII, Volume 5, 1531–1532, n. 1187.
[11] *Calendar of State Papers, Spain,* Volume 4 Part 2, 1531-1533, n. 998.
[12] Eric Ives, *The Life and Death of Anne Boleyn*, pp. 159-160.
[13] *Letters and Papers, Foreign and Domestic, Henry VIII,* Volume 6, 1533, n. 1331. *Letters and Papers, Foreign and Domestic, Henry VIII,* Volume 13 Part 2, August-December 1538, n. 804.
[14] *Letters and Papers, Henry VIII,* Volume 5, n. 1538.
[15] Ibid., n. 230.
[16] Catherine Fletcher, *Our Man in Rome*, p. 190, 191.
[17] *Letters and Papers, Henry VIII,* Volume 6, 1533, n. 585.
[18] Ibid., n. 1386.
[19] Paul Friedmann, *Anne Boleyn*, Volume 1, pp. 258-259.
[20] *Calendar of State Papers, Spain,* Volume 4 Part 2, 1531-1533, n. 1165.
[21] *Chronicle of King Henry VIII (The Spanish Chronicle),* p. 42.
[22] *Letters and Papers, Henry VIII,* Volume 7, 1534, n. 469.

Chapter 10: "Very expert in French tongue"

In 1534, Henry VIII decided to postpone another intended meeting with Francis I; the two Kings were to meet in Calais for a third time, but they never did. Henry instructed his ambassador, Anne Boleyn's younger brother, George, to use Marguerite, Queen of Navarre, as an intermediary. The ambassador was to tell the French King's sister that it was Anne who wished to defer the interview because she was unable to leave England on account of her advanced pregnancy and desired to have Henry at her side when her child was born. The ambassador was also to tell Marguerite that there was nothing Anne regretted more than the fact that she and the Queen of Navarre did not meet in Calais in 1532.[1]

Henry VIII decided to use this woman-to-woman approach because some sort of a relationship between Anne Boleyn and the French King's sister had developed during Anne's sojourn in France. The sixteenth-century biographer William Camden claimed that Anne served as

Marguerite's maid of honour after Queen Claude's death in 1524, but this served Camden's agenda of portraying Anne as the patroness of the reformed Church because Marguerite, he emphasised, "was a prime favourer of the Protestant religion then springing up in France".[2] Camden was clearly mistaken because Anne came back to England two years before Queen Claude's death.

It is certain, however, that she would have seen Marguerite on a daily basis at court and, just as she had formed an acquaintance with Madame Renée, Claude's sister, she had a chance to develop a relationship with the French King's sister. Just what sort of a relationship it was is hard to define due to the paucity of evidence. When the intended meeting between Henry VIII and Francis I was cancelled altogether, Anne confessed to one of Marguerite's messengers that her greatest wish, next to having a son, was to see Marguerite again.[3]

Marguerite clearly supported Anne's elevation to queenship. When Anne's uncle, the Duke of Norfolk, was sent to France as a special envoy in June 1533, he was under the impression that Marguerite was Henry VIII's and Anne Boleyn's "good and sure friend" and as affectionate as if she were their sister.[4] On Anne's accession, Marguerite sent congratulations and "very humble recommendations" to the new Queen of England.[5] Another piece of evidence supporting the friendly relationship between Anne and Marguerite is the book Francis I and Marguerite sent to Anne and Henry. It was comprised of a lengthy poem presumably authored by Clément Marot and included Anne Boleyn's device and her coat of arms. The poem touchingly addressed Anne with a prophecy that Christ would give her a son, "the living image of the King his father", whom they both would see grow into manhood.[6] The longed-for son never came, but some seven years after Anne Boleyn's death, her daughter, Elizabeth, translated Marguerite's poem, *Mirror of a Sinful Soul*, from French into English; it's believed that Anne owned a copy of this poem, published in 1531, and her daughter was well aware of the connection between the Queen of Navarre and her own mother.[7]

Anne was an avid collector of French theological books. William Latymer, her chaplain, recorded that Anne "was very expert in the French tongue, exercising herself continually in reading the French Bible and other French books of like effect".[8] She owned a copy of the French translation of the Bible by the humanist Jacques Lefèvre d'Étaples, translated in 1525 and printed in Antwerp in 1534. She also owned d'Étaples's *Epistles and Gospels for the*

52 Weeks of the Year. Both works were deemed heretical and condemned by the Sorbonne.

It is clear that the French King's sister was Anne's role model when it came to religion and patronage. Marguerite was the first source of information about reform for Anne Boleyn, and Anne's later religious views neatly correspond with those of Marguerite's. Just like Marguerite, Anne sought the correction of major abuses within the Church. Both women believed in making the Bible available to everyone in the vernacular and thus encouraged its translation. Anne and Marguerite were recognised as loyal promoters of the reformed religion and people often turned to them for help. Anne Boleyn helped at least two French religious refugees during her tenure as Queen. Her chaplain, William Latymer, described how she sheltered a certain "Mistress Marye", a French gentlewoman who sought refuge in England:

"As for an example, a gentlewoman of France named Mrs Marye[9] fled out of France into England for religion. Whom immediately after her arrival the Queen Her Majesty sent for, and understanding the certainty of the matter, entertained her so lovingly and honourably as she confessed that her trouble had purchased her liberty, and that she gained more by her banishment than she could have hoped for at home amongst her dear friends and natural countrymen of France."[10]

There was also Nicolas Bourbon, a French poet and Protestant who was maintained at Anne's expense in Dr William Butts's house. He hailed from Champagne and had Marguerite of Navarre as his patroness before he decided to flee to England in 1535 when religious persecution in France became so fierce that even the French King's sister had no power to help him. Bourbon returned to France shortly after Anne's death, but he never forgot her hospitality. In his collection of verses entitled *Nugae* (*Trifles*), he included laudatory poems addressed to Anne Boleyn, William Butts and other members of the evangelical circle at Henry VIII's court, including Thomas Cranmer and Thomas Cromwell, but it was Anne who was the most prominent in these verses.

However, neither the similarities between Marguerite of Navarre and Anne Boleyn nor Anne's efforts on behalf of French religious refugees were enough to restore good relations between England and France. By 1534, England had become isolated on the international political stage. Henry VIII's break from Rome naturally meant that any alliance between him and Charles V was impossible as long as Henry kept his first wife, Charles's aunt Katharine of Aragon, away from court. While Charles V would only ally with Henry if he took Katharine back as his wife, Henry was eager to seek the recognition of his marriage with Anne Boleyn and thus decided to ally with Francis I.

In the autumn of 1534, a mission from the French King headed by the Admiral of France, Philippe de Chabot, seigneur de Brion, came to England. Its main goal was to negotiate the marriage between one of Francis I's sons to Princess Elizabeth, or so Henry VIII believed. The admiral's treatment of Anne Boleyn was cold, and he went to see her only after the King asked if he wished to visit her. Then the admiral proposed a marriage between the French dauphin and Henry VIII's daughter by Katharine of Aragon, Mary, who had been recently excluded from succession and proclaimed a bastard. Both Henry and Anne were shocked at this proposal, and the King later complained to the admiral that "Francis could not have spoken seriously of that affair, but merely by way of a joke". The fact that Francis desired to marry his eldest son and heir to Katharine of Aragon's daughter meant that he, as most of the Catholic rulers in Europe, believed that Mary was legitimate and Elizabeth was not. Anne was not only "exceedingly annoyed" at this, but she soon became fearful that the King might abandon her.[11]

She had great reason to worry because the son who would consolidate her position as Queen had not yet been born. Just as Katharine of Aragon before her, Anne had given birth to a healthy daughter but struggled to deliver a male heir. The pregnancy that served as an excuse for annulling the French interview ended in mysterious circumstances during the summer progress of 1534. Whatever happened that fateful summer was kept secret, but various stories leaked, and soon rumours started swirling in the English countryside that Anne "had one child by the King, which was dead-born, and she prayed she might never have other".[12]

When the French admiral's secretary, Palmedes Gontier, arrived to England in February 1535, he recorded Anne Boleyn's insecurities in the following letter:

"She said the Admiral must think of applying some remedy, and act towards the King so that she may not be ruined and lost, for she sees herself very near that and in more grief and trouble than before her marriage. She charged him to beg the Admiral to consider her affairs, of which she could not speak as fully as she wished, on account of her fears, and the eyes which were looking at her, her husband's and the lords' present. She said she could not write, nor see him again, nor stay longer. She then left him, the King going to the next room, where the dance was beginning, without the said Lady going thither."[13]

Despite this, Henry VIII was still committed to Anne. In stipulations of the newly proposed treaty with France, he emphasised that Francis should acknowledge Henry's marriage to her as lawful and their offspring as legitimate.[14] In May 1535, the previously cancelled conference between England and France was held in Calais. This time it was an all-male assembly, but Henry VIII and Francis I did not appear in person, instead being represented by their selected ambassadors. Henry was represented by George Boleyn and Thomas Howard, and Francis had chosen Admiral de Brion. There was no understanding reached during the meeting.

When the English envoys returned home, Anne Boleyn received firsthand information about the negotiations from her brother who had a long discussion with her before reporting to the King himself. Both Anne and Henry desired that Francis I's son Charles, Duke of Angoulême, should marry their daughter, Elizabeth, and come to live and be educated at the English court prior to the marriage, yet Francis strongly opposed this idea, saying that he would not send his son to be a hostage in England. Francis's indignation with Henry deepened when the English envoys were heard saying that Henry VIII alleged that Francis had promised to send his son to England, yet the French King recalled no such promise.[15]

It was around that time when Francis told the papal nuncio that Henry VIII was "the hardest friend to bear in the world; at one time unstable, and at another time obstinate and proud, so that it was almost impossible to bear with him". He complained that Henry treated him like his subject—indeed, the English King demanded that Francis adopt the same anti-papal policy in France—and was afraid that he could "do no good with him" yet was prepared to put up with him because it was "no time to lose friends".[16] However, the French admiral broke off the negotiations "on account of his refusal to allow the Duke of Angoulême to go to England until the girl [Elizabeth] was old enough to be married and because he would not declare in any way against the Church, or in favour of the King's second wife".[17] He was also "sick of his mission . . . on account of the haggling and carping of the English".[18] Disappointed and angry, Anne Boleyn was soon publicly uttering unfavourable comments about Francis I and the

French nation as a whole. When the new French ambassador Antoine de Castelnau arrived in England in June 1535, Anne snubbed him when she deliberately failed to invite him for a splendid banquet she held at her palace of Hanworth.[19] Still, Anne made "frequent importunities", inviting the French ambassadors to visit Elizabeth and pay their respects to her.[20]

Additionally, Anne and Henry were perplexed when they learned that Mary of Hungary, who replaced Margaret of Austria as regent of the Netherlands, was to meet at Cambrai with Francis I's wife, Eleanor. Initially, the two women were to meet "for friendship of kindred", but since they were sisters and held influential positions at European courts, it was presumed that they would try to reconcile their brother Charles V with Francis I.[21] Rumours about her nieces' meeting prompted Katharine of Aragon to write to Mary of Hungary to beg her to help further her cause with the emperor. Knowing that Henry VIII was always desirous to build bridges with Francis I, Katharine also asked Mary to intercede with Eleanor on her behalf and "use her influence with the King her husband to be a good friend to Henry in getting him to abandon the sin in which he stands".[22] The meeting eventually took place in the summer of 1535, but it was not as politically significant as many expected.

By 1536, Henry VIII and Anne Boleyn had great reason to rejoice because Anne was pregnant again, and her rival, Katharine of Aragon, had died on 7 January 1536. Henry VIII was heard saying that he could now reconcile with Charles V because Katharine, who was the reason for the discord between them, was gone. He also instructed his ambassadors in France to be more aloof in dealings with Francis I.[23] Anne's pregnancy gave Henry hope of finally having a male heir, but by February 1536 Anne had miscarried a son, and Henry was so disappointed that he started entertaining doubts as to the validity of his marriage to her. "I see that God will not give me male children", he uttered to Anne when he visited her after the miscarriage.[24]

Anne's influence began to wane, and Henry found a new mistress in the person of Jane Seymour, one of Anne's maids of honour. Anne knew that her only chance of getting Henry's favour back was to give him a son and accept his political choices. In the spring of 1536, she reverted to anti-French policy when she was heard uttering unfavourable remarks about Francis I and willingly agreed to accept the alliance with Charles V.[25] She must have been aware that Francis was spreading unfavourable reports about her in his country. In March 1536, for instance, he revealed to the papal nuncio that Anne—"that woman", as he coldly referred to her—was not really with child but pretended to have miscarried a son.[26]

During his official visit to court in April 1536, Imperial ambassador Chapuys was invited by Thomas Cromwell to visit Anne and kiss her to acknowledge her as queen on Charles V's behalf. This took Chapuys by surprise because he never accepted Anne Boleyn as Queen and was already heavily involved with her enemies, plotting her downfall. He replied that although he was eager to please the King, "such a visit would not be advisable".[27] And yet Chapuys knew that meeting face-to-face with Anne Boleyn was inevitable. The two met after the Mass; Chapuys bowed to Anne when she and the King were leaving and she returned the reverence. This was not, however, the official acknowledgment Anne was anticipating.

On that same day Chapuys heard that Anne was no longer pro-French:

"Nevertheless, another courtier affirms that he heard the concubine [Anne] say to the King after dinner, that it was a great shame for the king of France to treat his own uncle, the duke of Savoy, as he was doing, and make preparations for the invasion of Milan for no other purpose, as she said, than to prevent and mar the enterprise against the Turk, and that it seemed as if the Most Christian King, weary of life owing to his sufferings and bad health, wished to put an end to his days as soon as possible."[28]

Anne now gravitated towards the imperial alliance, but Charles V was willing to accept Henry VIII as an ally only if he restored his daughter Mary to the succession. This meant that the elder Mary would take precedence over her younger half sister Elizabeth, who, in Charles's eyes, was merely a bastard. Henry was not about to allow the emperor to interfere in his family matters and scolded his ambassador in the presence of the whole court. This development frightened Thomas Cromwell, the King's right-hand man, who now believed that Anne Boleyn was an obstacle to their foreign policy and had to be removed from power. Cromwell reasoned that with Anne gone, Henry would be able to put the controversy of his divorce and subsequent remarriage behind him and start afresh.

NOTES

[1] *Letters and Papers, Henry VIII*, Volume 7, 1534, n. 958.

[2] William Camden, *The History of the Princess Elizabeth Late Queen of England*, p. 3.
[3] *Letters and Papers, Henry VIII*, Volume 9, August-December 1535, n. 378.
[4] *Letters and Papers, Henry VIII*, Volume 6, 1533, n. 692.
[5] Pierre Jourda, *Correspondance de Marguerite d'Angouleme*, p. 127.
[6] Eric Ives, *The Life and Death of Anne Boleyn*, p. 273.
[7] Susan Snyder, *Guilty Sisters*, p. 443.
[8] *William Latymer's Cronickille of Anne Bulleyne*, Volume 39 of Camden Fourth Series, p. 56.
[9] Her identity remains unknown.
[10] *William Latymer's Cronickille of Anne Bulleyne*, Volume 39 of Camden Fourth Series, p. 56.
[11] *Calendar of State Papers, Spain*, Volume 5 Part 1, 1534-1535, n. 112, 118.
[12] *Letters and Papers, Henry VIII*, Volume 8, n. 196.
[13] Ibid., n. 174.
[14] Ibid., n. 340.
[15] Ibid., n. 846.
[16] Ibid., n. 837.
[17] Ibid., n. 909.
[18] Ibid., n. 847.
[19] Ibid., n. 826, 876.
[20] Ibid., n. 594.
[21] Ibid., n. 1071.
[22] Ibid., Volume 9, n. 48.
[23] Ibid., Volume 10, n. 359, 760.
[24] Ibid., n. 351.
[25] Ibid., n. 699.
[26] Ibid., n. 450.
[27] Ibid., n. 699.
[28] Ibid., n. 699.

Chapter 11: "French bringing up and manners"

On 2 May 1536, Queen Anne was taken by barge to the Tower of London and accused of multiple counts of adultery, incest with her brother, George, and plotting Henry VIII's death; all this constituted treason. There was no truth to these allegations. The four men accused of being Anne's paramours—Henry Norris, Francis Weston, William Brereton and musician Mark Smeaton—were courtiers who had daily access to her chambers and were often seen in her company. Anne's recent quarrel with Henry Norris was taken out of context and twisted in its meaning; Weston told the Queen that Norris was frequenting her chambers because he fancied her and not Anne's cousin and Norris's fiancée, Mary Shelton. Anne scolded Norris for his tardiness in marrying her pretty cousin, accusing him for looking for "a dead man's shoes, for if aught came to the King but good, you would look to have me".[1] This was a dangerous thing to say, for it was treason to predict the King's death. Anne realised her foolish mistake the next day when she sent her chaplain to Norris so that he could swear that she was a good woman and there was no malicious intent in what she said, but it was too late. Rumours spread like wildfire within the claustrophobic confines of the court, setting hostile tongues wagging.

Anne's enthusiasm for all things French proved to be her undoing. She was distancing herself from the French alliance in the last months of her life, but her household was still managed in the French fashion characterized by the mingling of the sexes. In 1559, Scottish reformer Alexander Ales who was at court during Anne's downfall, wrote to Queen Elizabeth I that Anne had been accused of hosting dancing parties in her bedchamber, albeit with her chamberlains present.[2] A letter was produced against Anne and George, according to Ales, wherein Anne informed her brother that she was expecting a child.[3] The contents of the letter are unknown, and so the way Anne announced and discussed her pregnancy with George cannot be gauged. However, if she took example from the French noblewomen whom she served, Anne would have been very open about her condition. Marguerite of Navarre once wrote to the Grand Master of France about the fact that her period was late and she took it as a sign that she was pregnant but dared not to announce it just yet.[4]

Cromwell seized his opportunity and decided to strike against the Queen, accusing her of "incontinent living" and intimidating her ladies-in-waiting into confessing the names of other gallants who frequented Anne's chambers.[5] Crucial evidence, however, came from Anne herself. While pacing her royal apartments in the Tower, she nervously talked to her four female attendants, recalling her conversations with Henry Norris, Francis Weston and Mark Smeaton; these women were ordered to spy on the distraught Queen and inform Cromwell of everything she said. When Anne finally learned of the charges laid against her, she protested her innocence and said that no one could bring witnesses against her misconduct because she was not guilty.

Indeed, the bewildered imperial ambassador Eustace Chapuys recorded that no witnesses were brought against Anne or her brother during their separate trials, as was custom when the accused denied their guilt. Thomas Cromwell's letter to the English ambassadors at the French court—hungry for details and anxiously urging him to provide more information—reveals that evidence so painstakingly collected against the Queen was flimsy because "the very confessions . . . were so abominable that a great part of them were never given in evidence but clearly kept secret".[6] Chapuys, a skilled lawyer himself, was shocked that Anne and her alleged lovers "were sentenced on mere presumption or on very slight grounds, without legal proof or valid confession".[7] Only Mark Smeaton confessed to have had three sexual encounters with Anne, but he may have been tortured; historical sources are not unanimous on this issue. Thomas Cromwell later told Chapuys that the King ordered him to get rid of his Queen.

The four men co-accused with Anne Boleyn were executed on 17 May 1536. Anne faced death two days later. She addressed the crowds with the following words:

"Good Christian people, I have not come here to preach a sermon; I have come here to die. For according to the law and by the law, I am judged to die, and therefore I will speak nothing against it. I am come hither to accuse no man, nor to speak of that whereof I am accused and condemned to die, but I pray God save the King and send him long to reign over you, for a gentler nor a more merciful prince was there never, and to me he was ever a good, a gentle and sovereign lord. And if any person will meddle of my cause, I require them to judge the best. And thus I take my leave of the world and of you all, and I heartily desire you all to pray for me."[8]

When she knelt on a wooden scaffold draped in black cloth and covered with straw, one of her ladies-in-waiting stepped forward and bandaged her eyes. Anne prayed fervently, constantly turning her head back as if afraid the swordsman of French-held Calais, ordered especially for her execution, would slice through her neck without warning. "Oh, Lord, have mercy on me, to God I commend my soul, Jesus receive my soul", she kept repeating in prayer. The stroke was clean and swift; the French executioner charged £23 for the job well done.

Chronicler Edward Hall wrote that on Ascension Day, 4 June 1536, Henry VIII "wore white for mourning".[9] The colours of mourning in England were black and deep blue, never white. The fact that the King wore white to mourn Anne was because he wanted to highlight her French connection, as white was the colour of royal mourning in France.

Shortly after Anne's execution, Lancelot de Carle, a secretary to the French ambassador Antoine de Castelnau, penned a poem about her life and tragic death. De Carle was clearly very well informed because many of his assertions were confirmed by other contemporary sources. It is Lancelot de Carle who gives Anne a voice that reaches us across the centuries; he tells us about her eloquent trial speeches, where Anne said, among other things:

"I do not say that I always borne towards the King the humility which I owed him, considering his kindness and the great honour he showed me and the great respect he always paid me; I admit, too, that often I have taken it into my head to be jealous of him . . . But may God be my witness if I have done him any other wrong."[10]

This and other bold assertions uttered by Anne and her co-accused reached the Continent thanks to Lancelot de Carle, and soon many people abroad started believing that they were all unjustly condemned to die. When Henry VIII learned that "the French book, written in form of a tragedy" authored by "one [de] Carle, attendant upon the French ambassador" was being disseminated in France, he immediately ordered a copy for himself from his ambassador. Henry was not pleased with what he read, perhaps because most of it was true, but mostly because it was written in England under his very own royal nose.[11] Yet Henry could do nothing about the fact that Anne Boleyn's life and death was slowly turning into a legend. Two years after her execution, Étienne Dolet—another Frenchman—wrote an epitaph for "the Queen of Utopia" falsely accused of adultery by a tyrant of a husband.[12]

Historians could never satisfactorily explain why Henry VIII turned against Anne Boleyn and signed her death warrant. It has been recently proposed that he became a suspicious tyrant because of a personality change following a serious jousting accident. The accident occurred at a tournament at Greenwich Palace on 24 January 1536 when the forty-four-year-old King, in full armour, was thrown from his horse, itself armoured, which then fell on top of him. Dr Ortiz, the emperor's ambassador in Rome, recorded that in France Francis I was heard saying that Henry was unconscious for two hours, but no eyewitness mentioned this fact—not even the usually well-informed imperial ambassador Chapuys.[13] Henry survived, but the accident ended his jousting career and aggravated serious leg problems that plagued him for the rest of his life. It is also believed that the accident may well have caused a brain injury that profoundly affected the King's personality because, from 1536 onwards, Henry VIII became more suspicious, more tyrannical and more paranoid than ever before.[14] If Henry VIII's accident in 1536 did not change his personality, it certainly convinced him that he desperately needed a male heir. Beheading Anne Boleyn was one of the steps towards achieving that goal.

The day after Anne Boleyn's execution, the French ambassador rushed to Henry VIII's private chambers to propose a new marriage treaty. Francis I desired Henry VIII to marry his own daughter, the sixteen-year-old Madame Madeleine. The match was vigorously approved by the pope, who saw it as the most effectual way of convincing the English King to return to the Catholic Church.[15] Henry protested. He would not marry Madame Madeleine because she was "too young for him", and besides, he already had "too much experience of French bringing up and manners", alluding to the late Anne Boleyn.[16] He also added that he preferred to marry an Englishwoman because he could punish her if she misbehaved. Anne's devotion to France was well known in the Netherlands, where Mary of Hungary, who replaced the late Margaret of Austria as regent, had condemned Anne as "a good Frenchwoman", although Anne leaned towards the imperial alliance towards the end of her life.[17]

Henry VIII's marriage to Jane Seymour ("a good imperialist", according to Mary of Hungary) ended when the Queen died of childbed fever on 24 October 1537 after giving birth to Henry's longed-for son, Prince Edward. The King remarried three more times and died on 28 January 1547, aged fifty-five. He outlived Anne Boleyn by eleven years. On his deathbed, Henry expressed "peculiar remorse for the wrong he had done Anne Boleyn by putting her to death on a false accusation". This was recorded by the contemporary Franciscan French monk André Thevet, who resided in England at that time.[18]

All three of Henry VIII's children ascended to the throne: Prince Edward as Edward VI in 1547, Lady Mary in 1553 and Lady Elizabeth, Anne's daughter, in 1558. Anne's French sympathies were still remembered during Queen Mary's reign, when Mary said that she feared that Elizabeth would "imitate her mother in being a French partisan".[19]

NOTES

[1] Eric Ives, *The Life and Death of Anne Boleyn*, p. 335.
[2] *Calendar of State Papers Foreign: Elizabeth, Volume 1, 1558-1559,* n. 1303 (25, 28).
[3] Ibid., 1303 (28).
[4] Patricia F. Cholakian and Rouben C. Cholakian, *Marguerite de Navarre: Mother of the Renaissance*, p. 141.
[5] Roger B. Merriman, *Life and Letters of Thomas Cromwell,* Volume 2, p. 12.
[6] Ibid., p. 21.
[7] *Calendar of State Papers, Spain,* Volume 5 Part 2, 1536-1538, n. 55.
[8] Raphael Holinshed, *Holinshed's Chronicles of England, Scotland and Ireland*, Volume 3, p. 797.
[9] Edward Hall, Chronicle, p. 894.
[10] Eric Ives, *The Life and Death of Anne Boleyn*, p. 341.
[11] *Letters and Papers, Henry VIII,* Volume 12 Part 2, n. 78.
[12] Paul Friedmann, *Anne Boleyn: A Chapter of English History (1527-1536),* Volume 2, p. 300.
[13] *Letters and Papers, Henry VIII,* Volume 10, n. 427.

[14] Read more in Suzannah Lipscomb's *1536: The Year That Changed Henry VIII*, Lion Hudson, 2009.
[15] Paul Friedmann, *Anne Boleyn,* Volume 2, pp. 305-307.
[16] *Calendar of State Papers, Spain,* Volume 5 Part 2, 1536-1538, Additions and Corrections, n. 61.
[17] *Letters and Papers Henry VIII,* Volume 10, n. 965.
[18] Agnes Strickland, *Lives of the Queens of England*, Volume 2, p. 271.
[19] *Calendar of State Papers, Spain,* Volume 11, 28 November 1553.

Chapter 12:
"Le Royne Anne sans tête"

Shortly before her execution, Anne quipped that her enemies would nickname her "Le Royne Anne sans tête", "Queen Anne the Lackhead", and then "laughed heartily" as she did many times during her imprisonment.[1] In her last moments, she may have pondered over the words Margaret of Austria wisely wrote and shared with her female servants:

> "Trust in those who offer you service,
>
> And in the end, my maidens,
>
> You will find yourselves in the ranks of those
>
> Who have been deceived.
>
> They, for their sweet speeches, choose
>
> Words softer than the softest of virgins;
>
> Trust in them?
>
> In their hearts they nurture
>
> Much cunning in order to deceive,

And once they have their way thus,

Everything is forgotten.

Trust in them?"[2]

Indeed, in the end Anne found herself "in the ranks of those who have been deceived".[3] Betrayed by her royal husband and ladies-in-waiting, who unwillingly provided false testimonials of her immoral life, she made her way to the scaffold with inner calmness although not without anxiety. She didn't know it at the time, but her daughter, Elizabeth, who was merely two years and eight months old, would become Queen regnant against all odds in 1558. Yet, even in death and with her daughter on the throne, Anne's reputation was still under attack. Elizabeth was young, illegitimate and Protestant, but, above all, she was a woman in a man's world. Anne's execution served as a reminder that Elizabeth was a bastard and perhaps not even Henry VIII's child. The attacks came from Anne's beloved France, where a "lewd" book appeared early in Elizabeth's reign besmirching Anne's reputation. The book was "devised by a Frenchman, and printed at Lyons, wherein he has spoken most irreverently of the Queen's mother".[4] Its author, Gabriel De Sacconay, compared Anne "to the heathen wives of Solomon" who influenced the biblical king to leave the one true God and follow his wives' pagan deities. Anne, De Sacconay asserted, was the sole reason of Henry VIII's defection from the Catholic Church. Henry VIII's marriage to her was "a foul matrimony, engendered by lust". He also compared Anne to the biblical queen Jezebel, wife of Ahab, King of Israel, who worshipped deities Baal and Asherah and who was killed when members of her own retinue threw her out of a window. De Sacconay asserted that, like Jezebel, Anne "met with the just punishment for her wickedness, being executed for adultery".[5]

Elizabeth immediately wrote to her ambassador in Paris, Nicholas Throckmorton, instructing him to ask Catherine de Medici, Queen Mother (who was fifteen when Francis I turned his back on the Anglo-French alliance in 1533), to suppress the publication of this derogatory pamphlet. The French King ordered De Sacconay "to alter the offensive passages in his book", but Elizabeth demanded that every single copy be destroyed and no further copies printed.[6] This proves that even though Elizabeth never officially cleared her mother's name from slander by issuing an Act of Parliament protesting Anne's innocence, she did care about Anne's good name and wouldn't allow anyone to tarnish her late mother's reputation.

NOTES

[1] *Letters and Papers,* Volume 10, n. 1070.
[2] Eric Ives, *The Life and Death of Anne Boleyn*, p. 21.
[3] Ibid.
[4] *Calendar of State Papers Foreign: Elizabeth, Volume 4,* 1561-1562, n. 395.
[5] Ibid., n. 498.
[6] Ibid., n. 532.

Appendix 1:
In which year was Anne Boleyn born?

There are two schools of thought regarding the year in which Anne Boleyn was born: it's either c. 1501 or c. 1507. This narrative, however, is outdated and does not reflect everything we know about Anne Boleyn's origins.

The c. 1507 is understandable as it appears in William Camden's biography of Elizabeth I dating to 1615.[1] Some other writers based their conclusions about Anne's birth on Camden. Jane Dormer, for instance, dictating her memoir to her secretary Henry Clifford in the early 1600s reflected that Anne was "not yet twenty-nine years of age" when she was executed in May 1536.[2] However, the 1507 date suggested by William Camden has long been refuted by historical opinion based on the following facts. Anne started court service in 1513 as maid of honour to Archduchess Margaret of Savoy. She wrote a letter to her father from Margaret's court, but the letter is undated. It is, historians agree, an epistle penned by a teenager rather than by a six- or seven-year-old child. The post of a maid in

Margaret's household was open to girls between thirteen and fourteen years old, and if Anne was born in 1507, she would have been a child of seven.[3]

Anne left Margaret of Savoy's court and joined the household of Princess Mary Tudor, Henry VIII's younger sister, who married Louis XII of France at Abbeville in October 1514. Shortly after the nuptials, Louis XII dismissed his wife's attendants, including the experienced Lady Guildford, and it seems unreasonable to assume that he would have allowed a seven-year-old girl to stay. Anne not only stayed with Mary Tudor but when Mary contracted a secret marriage with Charles Brandon, Duke of Suffolk, and left France with him in April 1515, Anne stayed at the French court as a servant to Claude of Valois, the new King's wife. Something must have recommended Anne for the post of a maid of honour if Claude noticed her and valued Anne enough to let her serve in her household. It is unlikely that Anne was a child of six or seven in 1514; rather, she must have been a teenager who already spoke fluent, if perhaps still somewhat flawed, French.

Thomas Boleyn moved from Blickling Hall in Norfolk to Hever Castle in Kent at some point after his father's death in October 1505. In May 1538, Thomas wrote to Cromwell that he had been living in Kent "these thirty-three years", meaning that he moved from Blickling to Hever in or around 1505.[4] We know that Anne was born in Norfolk and not in Kent, so that fact alone establishes her birth year sometime before or at the latest in 1505 and certainly not in 1507. How do we know Anne was born in Norfolk? Matthew Parker, her chaplain, said he was her "poor countryman".[5] Eric Ives explains in his biography of Anne that Parker was following the sixteenth century's usage where "country" meant "county" or district.[6] When Anne's father informed Cromwell that he lived in Kent for the past thirty-three years, he also used the term "country". In 1536, Thomas Boleyn wrote that his wife gave him "every year a child" before they moved to Hever in 1505.[7] Knowing that Anne was born in Norfolk and not in Kent, it follows that she was born in or before the year 1505 and not later. If she was born in 1507, as Camden stated, Matthew Parker would not have described himself as her "poor countryman" because they would have been born in different counties; Parker in Norfolk, Anne in Kent. The 1507 date does not align with the known facts of Anne's life.

The date of the marriage of Anne's parents is unknown; if we knew the exact date, we would at least have a vague idea of when Elizabeth Boleyn started having her children. As far as we know there were five of them:

Thomas, Henry, Mary, Anne and George. Elizabeth Boleyn's jointure was settled on her in the summer of 1501 so she was certainly married by then.[8] This is probably why the c. 1501 is suggested as the earliest possible year of Anne's birth. However, the fact that Elizabeth Boleyn's jointure was settled in the summer of 1501 does not mean that she did not already have at least one child before that date. Eric Ives suggests that if "we take Boleyn's memory literally, we may suppose a child in 1499, another in 1500, a third in 1501 and so on..."[9] It is thus not impossible to suggest that Anne was born before the year 1501.

In general terms, it is far more accurate to state that Anne was born between c. 1501 (the earliest confirmation of her parents' marriage) and c. October-December 1505 (the Boleyns moving to Hever Castle and Anne thus being born in Norfolk, as per Parker's statement) but it is not implausible that she would have been born before summer of 1501.

A controversy still lingers over the birth order of the Boleyn children, especially over the respective ages of Anne and her sister Mary. It is generally believed that Mary Boleyn was the eldest child born to Thomas and Elizabeth and therefore Anne's elder sister. In contemporary sources, Anne is often referred to as "Thomas Boleyn's daughter" or "one of the daughters" born to him; it is generally assumed that if she had been his elder daughter or the eldest child, it would have been reflected in the documents.[10] The strongest evidence that Anne was younger than Mary comes from Mary Boleyn's grandson George Carey, who argued that since he descended from the eldest daughter of Thomas Boleyn, he should inherit the earldom of Ormond.[11]

Only the year of birth of George Boleyn, Anne's brother, can be gleaned from primary source material. George Cavendish, who served as Cardinal Wolsey's gentleman usher, wrote in his poem *Metrical Visions* that George was about twenty-seven when he gained a place in the Privy Chamber. George lost his position in the Privy Chamber by January 1526 but was restored in 1529. It is not clear to which year Cavendish was referring; if to 1529, then George was born c. 1502; if to 1525-26 then he was born c. 1498-99.[12]

What is known for certain is that according to Thomas Boleyn's testimony, a child was born for every year of his marriage to Elizabeth Howard until the death of Thomas's father in October 1505. If we date the marriage as occurring in 1501, the earliest confirmation on record, then we could plausibly speculate that all five Boleyn children, including Anne, had been born between summer 1501 and autumn 1505.

NOTES

[1] William Camden, *The History of the Princess Elizabeth Late Queen of England*, p. 3.
[2] Clifford, *The Life of Jane Dormer, Duchess of Feria*, p. 80.
[3] Paget, *The Youth of Anne Boleyn*, Historical Research, Volume 54, Issue 130, pp. 162–170.
[4] *Letters and Papers, Foreign and Domestic, Henry VIII,* Volume 13 Part 1, n. 937.
[5] Ives, *The Life and Death of Anne Boleyn*, p. 367.
[6] Ibid.
[7] *Letters and Papers, Foreign and Domestic, Henry VIII,* Volume 11, n. 17.
[8] Ives, p. 17.
[9] Ibid.
[10] *Letters and Papers, Foreign and Domestic, Henry VIII,* Volume 3, n. 1011.
[11] Wilkinson, *Mary Boleyn: The True Story of Henry VIII's Favourite Mistress*, p. 11.
[12] Ives, p. 15.

APPENDIX 2:
WAS MARY BOLEYN FRANCIS I'S MISTRESS?

It is widely believed today that Mary Boleyn was the mistress of Francis I at some point during her stay at the French court. This notion is based on the French King's reminisce from 1536, when he boasted that he knew Mary Boleyn "here in France" as "una grandissima ribalda" which means more or less that she was notoriously infamous for her promiscuity. The whole report was recorded by Rodolfo Pio di Carpi, Bishop of Faenza, who stated that:

"Francis said also that they are committing more follies than ever in England, and are saying and printing all the ill they can against the Pope and the Church; that 'that woman' pretended to have miscarried of a son, not being really with child, and, to keep up the deceit, would allow no one to attend on her but her sister, whom the French king knew here in France 'per una grandissima ribalda et infame sopre tutte' ["a great wanton and notoriously infamous"]."[1]

This report is wrong on many levels. First, "that woman", Anne Boleyn, was indeed pregnant and did not pretend to have miscarried a son—she really did miscarry a foetus that had the appearance of a male, at about fifteen weeks' gestation, as recorded by a contemporary chronicler.[2] It looks like the Bishop of Faenza was referring to Anne and not Mary when he made a comment about "that woman... whom the King knew here in France." There is no indication in the report that Francis was referring to knowing "that woman" carnally. There is also no tangible evidence that Mary Boleyn was back at court after she and her newly wedded husband, William Stafford, were banished for marrying in secret in 1534. Because of these glaring errors, the report is generally regarded with a touch of reserve when it comes to Anne Boleyn. Oddly, it is rarely questioned when it comes to Mary, and the Bishop of Faenza's words are often quoted to prove that Mary was Francis I's mistress because it is assumed that the French King "knew" Mary in the carnal sense.[3]

If Mary indeed slept with the French King, she would not be his mistress per se, as Francis had only two official mistresses during his reign.[4] Still, he kept a group of ladies known as his "petite bande" with whom he slept regularly. This "little band of the Court ladies" was comprised of "the handsomest, daintiest and most favoured" women of court.[5] They were not only the King's sex partners; he often took them to hunt, enjoyed reading and discussing poetry in their circle and invited them to banquets. If Mary was part of this circle, it was never recorded, and indeed it remains speculative whether Francis would have spoken in such a scathing manner about a woman who formed part of his much-favoured "petite bande". The only historian who challenged the view that Mary Boleyn was Francis I's mistress is Retha M. Warnicke, who pointed out that in 1514 Mary Boleyn was too young to achieve such notoriety and that Francis I may have well referred to the 1532 meeting in Calais and "come to this conclusion about her character at that time, aware that she was Henry's ex-mistress".[6]

In 1585, Nicholas Sander, in his The Rise and Growth of the Anglican Schism, asserted that Anne Boleyn was also known for promiscuity while in France:

"At fifteen she [Anne Boleyn] sinned first with her father's butler, and then with his chaplain, and forthwith was sent to France, and placed, at the expense of the King, under the care of a certain nobleman not far from Brie. Soon afterwards she appeared at the French court where she was called the English Mare, because of her shameless behaviour; and then the royal mule, when she became acquainted with the King of France."[7]

Nicholas Sander is a notoriously unreliable source, writing some forty-five years after Anne Boleyn's execution with one clear purpose of besmirching the reputations of Anne, her daughter, Queen Elizabeth, and the entire Boleyn clan. There is no evidence that Anne Boleyn or her sister acquired a notorious reputation while serving as maids of honour in France. If the Boleyn sisters were indeed as notorious for their promiscuity as Nicholas Sander and Rodolfo Pio di Carpi claimed, the rumours would have been circulating in England as well as in France, and it remains dubious whether Henry VIII would take one sister as his mistress and the other as his wife had they been so notorious.

It has been credibly suggested that the town of "Brie" mentioned by Sander is Briis-sous-Forges where a Donjon d'Anne Boleyn, Anne Boleyn's Tower, the only remnant of the castle that once loomed large over the village, still stands today. A plaque nearby states that Anne lived in the castle with the family of Du Moulin, and a local road is named in her honour. If Mary Boleyn was truly known as a sexually promiscuous young woman when she served in France, it may have been she who was sent to Briis-sous-Forges, as suggested by her recent biographer.[8]

NOTES

[1] *Letters and Papers,* Volume 10, n. 450.
[2] Charles Wriothesley, *A Chronicle of England During the Reigns of the Tudors*, Volume 1, p. 33.
[3] Alison Weir, *Mary Boleyn: The Great and Infamous Whore*, p. 69.
[4] Tracy Adams & Christine Adams, *The Creation of the French Royal Mistress: From Agnès Sorel to Madame Du Barry*, pp. 37-67.
[5] Pierre de Bourdeille Brantôme, *Illustrious Dames of the Court of the Valois Kings*, p. 52.
[6] Retha M. Warnicke, *Wicked Women of Tudor England*, p. 30.
[7] Nicholas Sander, *The Rise and Growth of Anglican Schism*, p. 25
[8] Alison Weir, *Mary Boleyn: The Great and Infamous Whore*, pp. 115-117.

Acknowledgments

I would like to offer special thanks to the archivists at the British Library, National Archives, Bibliothèque Nationale de France and Bibliothèque Abbé Grégoire in Blois. Special thanks to Professor Tracy Adams and Barbara Parker Bell, who read an advanced copy of this book before publication and so graciously provided a review.

As always, I thank my husband, whose love and support are the most important, for entertaining our children, cooking delicious meals and providing copious amounts of tea when I'm busy writing.

I thank my editor, Jenny Quinlan, from Historical Editorial for her invaluable skills. With each book, her exceptional editing skills and insightful feedback have transformed my initial drafts into masterpieces.

Last but not least, I thank my readers for the support I receive from you every day; you are the reason I do what I do. Your reviews, comments and messages on social media have brightened my writing days. I am endlessly grateful for the way you've welcomed my books into your hearts and homes.

PICTURE SECTION

Plate 1: Hever Castle as it looks today.

Plate 2: Thomas Boleyn, as depicted in his memorial brass at St Peter's Church near Hever Castle.

Plate 3: Margaret of Austria by Bernard van Orley.

Plate 4: The castle of Tervuren, Margaret of Austria's summer residence.

Plate 5: Charles, Prince of Castile and future Holy Roman Emperor.

Plate 6: Henry VIII as he looked in 1531.

Plate 7: Mary Tudor, Henry VIII's younger sister.

Plate 8: Louis XII of France, Mary Tudor's first husband.

Plate 9: Anne of Brittany, mother of Queen Claude.

Plate 10: Francis I in 1515.

Plate 11: Louise of Savoy, Francis's mother. Image from Catherine de Medici's prayer book.

Plate 12: The wedding portrait of Mary Tudor and Charles Brandon. The clothing style indicates that this is a posthumous depiction, perhaps from the 1540s.

Picture section

Plate 13: Château du Clos Lucé, where Italian painter Leonardo da Vinci spent his last years.

Plate 14: Chateau de Blois, where Anne served Queen Claude.

Plate 15: Chateau de Amboise, one of Francis I's favourite residences.

Plate 16: The tower of the castle of Briis-sous-Forges, where Anne Boleyn supposedly lived.

Picture section

Plate 17: The plaque stating that Anne lived in the Briis-sous-Forges castle.

Plate 18: Posthumous image of Queen Claude surrounded by her daughters: Louise, Charlotte, Marguerite and Madeleine. Francis I's second wife, Eleanor of Portugal, dressed in widow's weeds, stands in the background. Image from Catherine de Medici's prayer book. Wikimedia Commons.

Plate 19: Margaret of Angoulême, Queen of Navarre, c. 1527. This is the only extant portrait depicting Margaret in colourful, rich clothing. Four years later, she started wearing black for mourning after the death of her six-month-old son, Jean. Wikimedia Commons.

Plate 20: Anne Boleyn's signature from her music book. Wikimedia Commons.

Plate 21: Anne Boleyn immortalised in a medal from 1534. It was cast in lead when Anne was believed to be pregnant. It is the only undisputed likeness of the controversial Queen from her lifetime. Wikimedia Commons.

Selected Bibliography

Habsburg & Valois Courts

Manuscript sources:

Bibliothèque Abbé Grégoire:

Manuscrit des funérailles de Claude de France et Charlotte sa fille, Blois-Agglopolys, Fonds patrimonial, ms. 245.

Bibliothèque Nationale De France:

Etat de maison de Claude de France (1514-1515), ms.fr. 7853, f. 310.

Etat de maison de Claude de France (1518), ms.fr. 2940, f.48.

Etat de maison de Claude et Renee (1515-1515), ms.fr. 7853, f. 311-312.

Etat de maison de Marie, reine d'Angleterre, ms.fr. 7853, f. 305v.

Primary sources:

Barillon. *Journal de Jean Barrillon, secrétaire du Chancelier Duprat, 1515-1521*, ed. P. de Vaissière. Two Volumes, 1897-9.

Brantôme, P. de Bourdeille, abbé de. *The Book of the Ladies (Illustrious Dames)*, tr. Katharine Prescott Wormeley. Hardy, Pratt & Company, 1899.
Lives of Fair and Gallant Ladies. Two Volumes. The Alexandrian Society, Inc. London and New York, 1922.

Selected Bibliography

Briçonnet, G., and Marguerite d'Angoulême. *Correspondance (1521-1524)*, ed. C. Martineau and M. Veissière, Two Volumes. Librairie Droz, 1975.

Castiglione, B. *The Book of the Courtier*, tr. L. Eckstein Opdycke. Charles Scribner's Sons, 1901.

Catalogue des actes de François Ier, 10 Volumes. 1887-1910.

De Beatis, A. *The Travel Journal of Antonio De Beatis: Germany, Switzerland, the Low Countries, France and Italy, 1517-1518*, tr. J.R. Hale and J.M.A. Lindon, ed. J.R. Hale, London, 1979.

Florange. *Mémoires du maréchal de Florange, dit le Jeune Adventureaux*, ed. R. Goubaux and P. A. Lemoisne, Two Volumes. Librairie Renouard. Paris, 1913-24.

Génin, F. *Lettres de Marguerite d'Angoulême, Soeur de François 1er, Reine de Navarre.* Paris, 1841.

Gringore, P. *Les Entrées Royales à Paris de Marie d'Angleterre (1514) et Claude de France (1517)*, ed. C.J. Brown. Librairie Droz, 2005.

Jansen, S. *Anne of France: Lessons for My Daughter*.Cambridge: D.S. Brewer, 2004.

Jourda, P. *Correspondance de Marguerite d'Angouleme*. Slatkine Reprint, 1973.

Journal de Louise de Savoie, in *Nouvelle collection de mémoires pour servir à l'histoire de France*, 1st ser. vol. 4, 83-93, ed. J. F. Michaud and J.J.F. Poujoulat. Paris, 1851.

Journal d'un bourgeois de Paris sous le règne de François Ier, 1515-1536, ed. V.L. Bourrilly, 1910.

Le Glay, A.J.C. *Négociations diplomatiques entre la France et l'Autriche*, Two Volumes, Paris, 1845.

Secondary sources:

Adams, Christine and Adams, Tracy. *The Creation of the French Royal Mistress: From Agnès Sorel to Madame Du Barry.* Penn State University Press, 2020.

Ambrière, F. *Le favori de François Ier, Gouffier de Bonnivet, Admiral de France; chronique des années 1489-1525,* Hachette, 1936.

Anderson, M.A. *St. Anne in Renaissance Music: Devotion and Politics.* Cambridge University Press, 2014.

Bapst, E. *Les Mariages de Jacques V.* Librairie Plon, 1889.
Benoit Rouard, E.A. *François Ier chez Mme De Boisy: Notice d'un recueil de crayons ou portraits aux crayons de couleur enrichi par le roi François Ier de vers et de devises inédites appartenant à la Bibliothèque Méjanes d'Aix.* A. Aubry, 1863.

Bertière, S. *Les Reines de France au Temps des Valois*, Two Volumes. Le Livre de Poche, 1996.

Brown, C.J. *The Cultural and Political Legacy of Anne de Bretagne: Negotiating Convention in Books and Documents.* D.S. Brewer Gallica, 2010.

The Queen's Library: Image-Making at the Court of Anne of Brittany, 1477-1514. University of Pennsylvania Press, 2011.

Cholakian, P.F., and Cholakian, R.C. *Marguerite de Navarre: Mother of the Renaissance.* Columbia University Press, 2006.

Cox Rearick, J. "Power-Dressing at the Courts of Cosimo de' Medici and François I: The "Moda alla Spagnola" of Spanish Consorts Eléonore d'Autriche and Eleonora di Toledo". *Artibus et Historiae*, Vol. 30, No. 60 (2009), pp. 39-69.

Croizat, Y.C. "'Living Dolls': François Ier Dresses His Women". *Renaissance Quarterly*, Vol. 60, No. 1 (Spring 2007), pp. 94-130.

Cullerier, A. *De quelle maladie est mort François Ier: Extrait de la Gazette hebdomadaire de médecine et de chirurgie.* Victor Masson, 1856.

De Boom, G. *Éléonore d'Autriche: Reine de Portugal et de France.* Bruxelles, 1995.

Dickman Orth, M. "Francis Du Moulin and the Journal of Louise of Savoy". *The Sixteenth Century Journal,* Vol. 13, No. 1 (Spring, 1982), pp. 55-66.

Freeman, J. F. "Louise of Savoy: A Case of Maternal Opportunism". *The Sixteenth Century Journal,* Vol. 3, No. 2 (Oct., 1972), pp. 77-98.

Héritier, J. *Catherine de Medici.* St Martin's Press, 1963.

Hourihane, C. *The Grove Encyclopaedia of Medieval Art and Architecture.* Volume 2. OUP USA, 2012.

Knecht, R.J. *Francis I.* Cambridge University Press, 1984.

Kolk, Caroline zum. "The Household of the Queen of France in the Sixteenth Century", *The Court Historian* 14, 1 (June 2009), pp. 3-22.

Lacroix, P. *Louis XII et Anne de Bretagne.* Hurtrel, 1802.

Matarasso, P.M. *Queen's Mate: Three Women of Power in France on the Eve of the Renaissance.* Ashgate, 2001.

Maulde-La Clavière, R. *Louise de Savoie et François Ier: Trente ans de Jeunesse (1485-1515).* Perrin et Cie, 1895.

Michael of Kent, P. *The Serpent and the Moon: Two Rivals for the Love of a Renaissance King.* Simon and Schuster, 2005.

Moulton Mayer, D. *The Great Regent: Louise of Savoy 1476-1531.* Wiedenfeld and Nicolson. 1966.

Noel Williams, H. *Henri II: His Court and Times.* Charles Scribner's Sons, 1910.

Noel Williams, H. *The Pearl of Princesses: The Life of Marguerite d'Angoulême, Queen of Navarre.* Eveleigh Nash Company, 1916.

Parker, G. *Emperor: A New Life of Charles V*. Yale University Press, 2019.

Pigaillem, H. *Claude de France, Première Épouse de François Ier*. Pygmalion, 2006.

Potter, D. *Henry VIII and Francis I: The Final Conflict, 1540-47*. Brill, 2011.

Potter, D. "Politics and faction at the court of Francis I: the duchesse d'Etampes, Montmorency and the Dauphin Henri". *French History*, July 2007, pp. 127–146.

Richardson, W.C. *Mary Tudor: The White Queen*. Owen, 1970.

Sadlack, E.A. *The French Queen's Letters: Mary Tudor Brandon and the Politics of Marriage in Sixteenth-Century Europe*. Palgrave Macmillan, 2011.

Sichel, E.H. *Catherine de Medici and the French Reformation*. Archibald Constable & CO, 1995.

Tremayne, E. *The First Governess of the Netherlands: Margaret of Austria*. Methuen, 1908.

Walker Freer, M. *The Life of Marguerite D'Angoulême: Queen of Navarre, Duchesse D'Alençon and de Berry, Sister of Francis I, King of France*. Two Volumes. Hurst and Blackett, 1854.

Wellman, K. *Queens and Mistresses of Renaissance France*. Yale University Press, 2013.

Whittaker, G.B. *The History of Paris from the Earliest Period to the Present Day: Containing a description of its antiquities, public buildings, civil, religious, scientific, and commercial institutions*. Paris: A. and W. Galignani, 1827.

English court

Primary sources:

Calendar of State Papers, Spain. Ed. Brewer, J.S. & Gairdner. J. Institute of Historical Research (1862-1932).

Camden, W. *The History of the Most Renowned and Victorious Princess Elizabeth Late Queen of England.* Flesher, 1688.

Cavendish, G. *The Life and Death of Cardinal Wolsey.* S.W. Singer, Harding and Leppard, ed. 1827.

Cranmer, T. *Miscellaneous Writings and Letters of Thomas Cranmer.* Ed. J.E. Cox for The Parker Society. University Press, 1846.

Ellis, H. *Original Letters Illustrative of English History,* Volume 2. (2nd series). Harding and Lepard, 1827.

Everett Wood, A. *Letters of Royal and Illustrious Ladies of Great Britain.* Three Volumes. London, H. Colburn, 1846.

Foxe, J. *The Actes and Monuments of the Church.* Ed. Hobart Seymour. M. Robert Carter & Brothers, 1855.

Giustiniani, S. *Four Years at the Court of Henry VIII.* Two Volumes. London, Smith, Elder, 1854, tr. Rawdon Brown.

Hall, E. *Hall's Chronicle.* J. Johnson, 1809.

Harris, N. *Proceedings and Ordinances of the Privy Council of England.* Volume 7. G. Eyre and A. Spottiswoode, 1837.

Latymer, W. "William Latymer's Cronickille of Anne Bulleyne". Ed. Maria Dowling, *Camden Miscellany,* xxx. Camden Soc. 4th ser. 39. 1990.

Letters and Papers, Foreign and Domestic, of the Reign of Henry VIII. 28 Volumes. Ed. Brewer, J.S. & Gairdner. J. Institute of Historical Research (1862-1932).

Sharp Hume, M.A. *Chronicle of King Henry VIII of England.* George Bell and Sons, 1889.

Pole, R. *Pole's Defense of the Unity of the Church.* Newman Press, 1965.

Sander, N. *Rise and Growth of the Anglican Schism.* Burns and Oates, 1877.

Wriothesley, C. *A Chronicle of England During the Reigns of the Tudors, from A.D. 1485 to 1559.* Camden Society, 1875.

Secondary sources:

Benger, E. *Memoirs of the Life of Anne Bolyn, Queen of Henry VIII.* Volume 2. Longman, Hurst, Rees, Orme, and Brown, 1821.

Bernard, G.W. "Did Anne Boleyn crave the crown?" *BBC History Magazine,* June 2015.

Brigden, S. "Henry Howard, Earl of Surrey, and the 'Conjured League'". *The Historical Journal*, Vol. 37, No. 3 (Sep., 1994), pp. 507-537.

Chalmers, C.R. and Chaloner, E.J. "500 years later: Henry VIII, leg ulcers and the course of history". *Journal of the Royal Society of Medicine,* 2009 Dec 1; 102(12): pp. 514–517.

De Lisle, L. *Tudor: A Family Story.* Vintage Digital, 2013. Kindle edition.

Evans, V.S. *Ladies-in-Waiting: Women Who Served at the Tudor Court.* CreateSpace Independent Publishing Platform, 2014.

Selected Bibliography

Everett Green, M.A. *Lives of the Princesses of England, from the Norman Conquest.* Volume 4. Longman, Brown, Green, Longman & Roberts, 1857.

Fletcher, C. *Our Man in Rome: Henry VIII and his Italian Ambassador.* Random House, 2012.

Friedmann, P. *Anne Boleyn: A Chapter of English History, 1527-1536.* Two Volumes. Macmillan and Co., 1884.

Gledhill Russell, J. *The Field of Cloth of Gold: Men and Manners in 1520.* Barnes & Noble, 1969.

Gristwood, S. *Blood Sisters: The Women Behind the Wars of the Roses.* Harper Press, 2012.

Hutchinson, R. *The Last Days of Henry VIII: Conspiracy, Treason and Heresy at the Court of the Dying Tyrant.* Phoenix, 2006.

Ives, E. W. *The Life and Death of Anne Boleyn: The Most Happy.* Blackwell Publishing, 2010.

Jones, P. *The Other Tudors Henry VIII's Mistresses and Bastards.* Metro Books, 2010.

Lingard, J. *The history of England, from the first invasion by the Romans to the accession of William and Mary in 1688.* Volume 4. C. Dolman, 1849.

Lipscomb, S. *1536: The Year that Changed Henry VIII.* Lion Hudson, 2009.

Merriman, R.B. *Life and Letters of Thomas Cromwell.* Two Volumes. Clarendon Press, 1902.

Norton, E. *Anne Boleyn: In Her Own Words & the Words of Those Who Knew Her.* Amberley Publishing, 2012.

Norton, E. *Bessie Blount: Mistress to Henry VIII.* Amberley Publishing, 2012.

Norton, E. *Jane Seymour: Henry VIII's True Love.* Amberley Publishing, 2010.

Norton, E. *The Boleyn Women: The Tudor Femmes Fatales Who Changed English History.* Amberley Publishing, 2013.

Scarisbrick, J.J. *Henry VIII.* Yale University Press, 2011.

Snyder, S. "Guilty Sisters: Marguerite de Navarre, Elizabeth of England, and the Miroir de l'âme Pécheresse". *Renaissance Quarterly*, Vol. 50, No. 2 (Summer, 1997), pp. 443-458.

Starkey, D. *Six Wives: The Queens of Henry VIII.* Vintage, 2004.

Strickland, A. *Lives of the Queens of England, from the Norman conquest.* Volume 2. London, 1864.

Urkevich, L. "Anne Boleyn, a music book, and the northern Renaissance courts: Music Manuscript 1070 of the Royal College of Music, London." PhD dissertation, University of Maryland, 1997.

Urkevich, L. "Anne Boleyn's French Motet Book, a Childhood Gift. The Question of the Original Owner of MS1070 of the Royal College of Music, London, Revisited" in *Ars musica septentrionalis*, PU Paris-Sorbonne, 2011.

Vincent, J.M. *The Life of Henry the Eighth and History of the Schism of England*, trans. Kirwan Browne, E.G. C. Dolman, 1852.

Walters Schmid, S. "Anne Boleyn, Lancelot de Carle, and the Uses of Documentary Evidence", PhD dissertation, Arizona State University, 2009.

Weir, A. *Mary Boleyn: 'The Great and Infamous Whore'.* Vintage, 2011.

Wilkinson, J. *Anne Boleyn: The Young Queen to Be.* Amberley Publishing, 2010.

Wilkinson, J. Mary Boleyn: The True Story of Henry VIII's Favourite Mistress. Amberley Publishing, 2009.

About the Author

Sylvia Barbara Soberton is a writer and researcher specialising in the history of the Tudors. She is best known for *The Forgotten Tudor Women* book series, which concentrates on shifting the perspective from famous figures like Henry VIII's six wives to the lesser-known, but no less influential, women of the Tudor court.

Sylvia has written ten books to date, and her newest titles include *Ladies-in-Waiting: Women Who Served Anne Boleyn* and *Medical Downfall of the Tudors: Sex, Reproduction & Succession*. Her ground-breaking research on the women who served Anne Boleyn was profiled in *Smithsonian Magazine, The Express* and *History of Scotland Magazine*. Sylvia is a regular contributor to the *Ancient Origins* website and magazine. She also talks about her books and research on podcasts such as *The Tudors Dynasty*, *Not Just the Tudors*, *Talking Tudors* and many more.

You can find Sylvia on

Facebook @theforgottentudorwomen

Instagram @forgottentudorwomen

and Twitter @SylviaBSo

Printed in Great Britain
by Amazon